BASIC SEWING

ESSENTIAL TIPS 101

BASIC SEWING

TECHNICAL CONSULTANT
Chris Jefferys

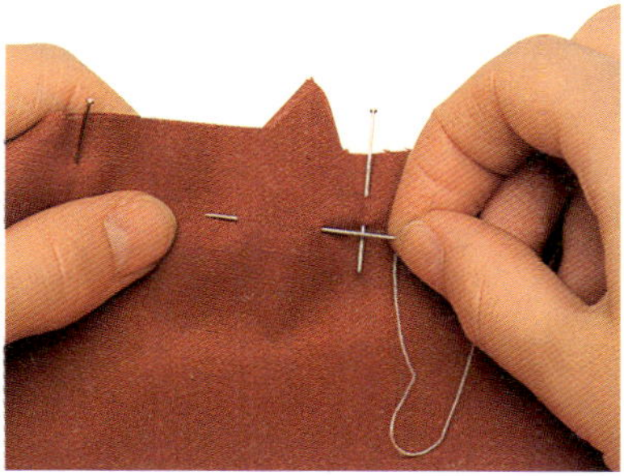

FENN

A DK PUBLISHING BOOK

Editor James Harrison
Art Editor Ted Kinsey
Senior Editor Gillian Roberts
Series Art Editor Alison Donovan
Production Controller Hélène Lamassoure
US Editor Laaren Brown

First published in Canada in 1997 by
Fenn Publishing Company Ltd.
34 Nixon Road, Bolton, Ontario, Canada, L7E 1W2

Visit Dorling Kindersley on the World Wide Web at http://www.dk.com

Published in Great Britain by Dorling Kindersley Limited.

Cataloguing in Publication Information is available from the National Library of Canada

ISBN 1-55168-130-7

Text film output by The Right Type, Great Britain
Reproduced by Colourscan, Singapore
Printed and bound in Italy by Graphicom

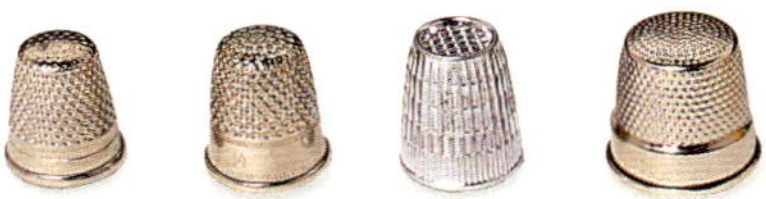

101 ESSENTIAL TIPS

The Tools You Need

1 Choosing Cutting Tools

Use sharp, high-grade steel cutting tools to avoid damaging fabrics. You'll need sewing scissors for trimming seams and facings; bent-handled shears for cutting out; embroidery scissors for needlework; pinking shears for fabrics that fray; and seam rippers to undo stitches.

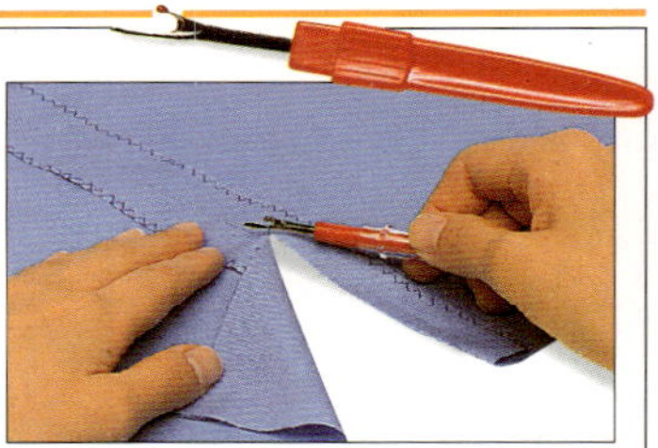

△ ***Seam ripper*** *has a sharp, curved hook to open seams and to cut buttonholes or stitches.*

▽ ***Bent-handled shears*** *are best for cutting out garments. The angled handles help you to cut but still leave the fabric flat.*

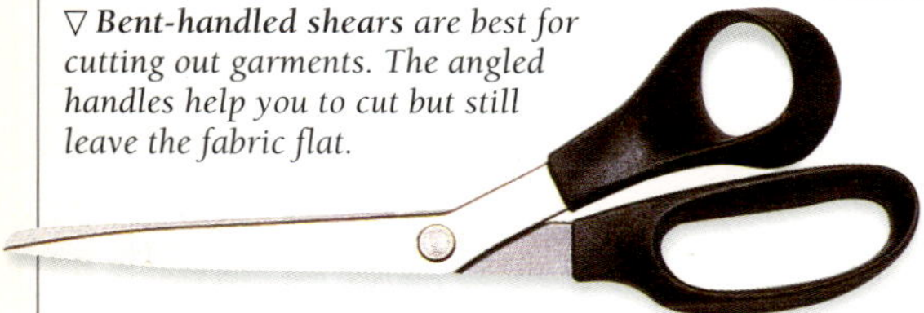

△ ***Embroidery scissors*** *have very sharp, pointed blades and so are ideal for needlework and buttonhole cutting.*

▽ ***Sewing scissors*** *have a blunt point on the upper blade to prevent the fabric from tearing.*

▷ ***Pinking shears,*** *with a zigzag blade, help finish raw edges on fabrics that will fray.*

2 MEASURING & MARKING TOOLS

You will need a tape measure to measure your body size and take pattern measurements, so you can make any necessary adjustments to get a good fit. To transfer pattern markings to garment fabric pieces, and for marking alterations, you should use a marking pen or pencil.

▷ ***Retractable tape measure*** *has a rolling mechanism to rewind the tape.*

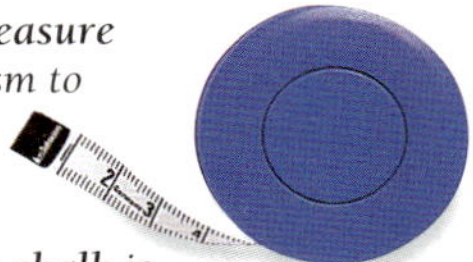

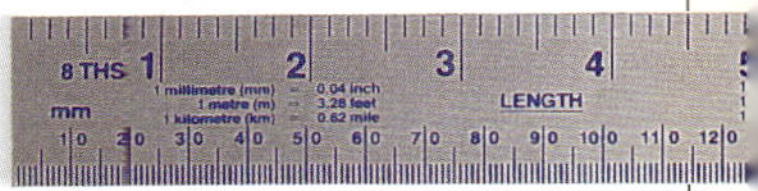

△ ***Measuring stick*** *is a straight stick for checking grainlines and marking hems.*

◁ ***Tailor's chalk*** *is available in many colors; remove it by brushing.*

△ ***Dressmaker's pencil,*** *with erasing brush, is for fine line marking.*

▽ ***Tailor's chalk pencil*** *is for marking details such as pleats or darts.*

△ ***Tape measure*** *has markings on both sides.*

▽ ***Sewing gauge*** *has sliding tabs to measure hems and pleats.*

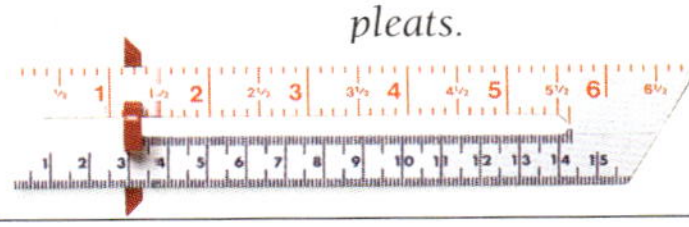

3 PINS & HAND-SEWING NEEDLES

Dressmaker's nickel-plated, brass, or stainless steel pins will cover most basting needs. Needles vary in size, length, and point shape for specific uses.

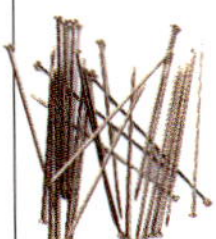

◁ ***Dressmaker's pins*** *are usually 1¹⁄₁₆in (26mm) long.*

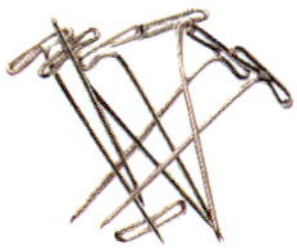

▷ ***Glass-headed pins*** *are easier to handle.*

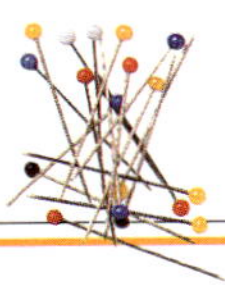

△ ***T-pins*** *stay in position on open-weave fabrics.*

Sharps *are widely used for general-purpose hand-sewing*

Straws, *also called milliner's needles, are ideal for basting*

Betweens, *short needles with a round eye, are used to make close, fine stitches*

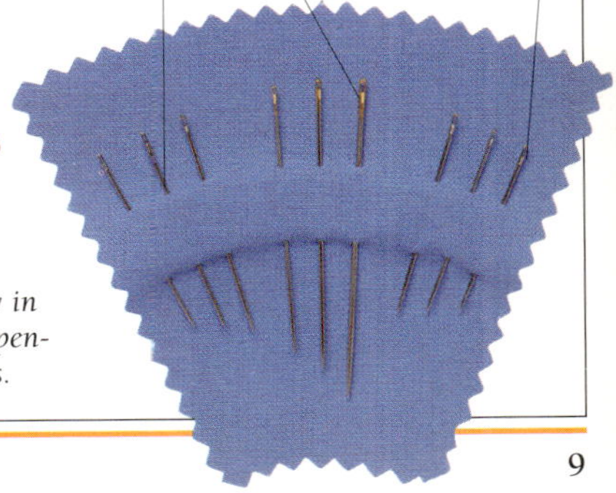

4 THIMBLES & THREADERS

Handy aids for safer, faster, and easier sewing, thimbles and threaders are usually plastic or metal. Thimbles come in various sizes to fit on the middle finger of the hand holding the needle. This enables you to push the needle through the fabric painlessly.

△ THIMBLES OF VARIOUS SIZES

◁ ***Needle threaders** have a wire at the end that pulls the thread through the eye of the needle.*

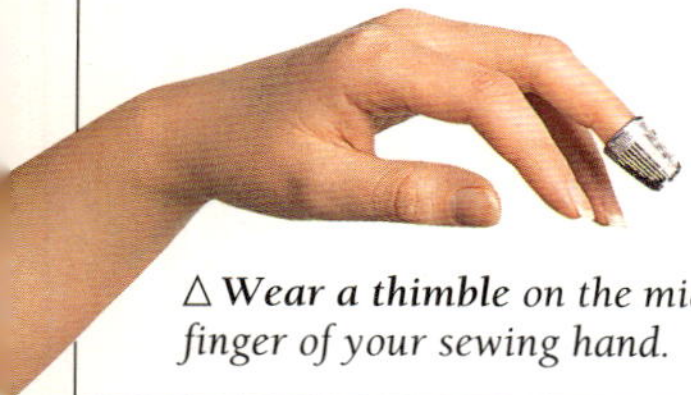

△ ***Wear a thimble** on the middle finger of your sewing hand.*

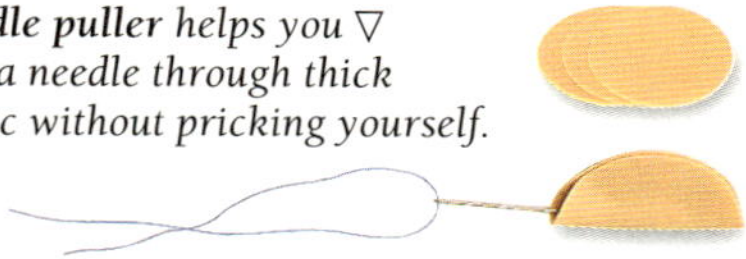

***Needle puller** helps you ▽ pull a needle through thick fabric without pricking yourself.*

5 PRESSING TOOLS

The essential pressing tool is a steam iron with an easy-to-use and effective steam trigger. The steam should come out in a noticeable surge. It is a mistake to economize on ironing boards, since cheaper versions break or wobble easily. You also need a pressing cloth for ironing delicate materials.

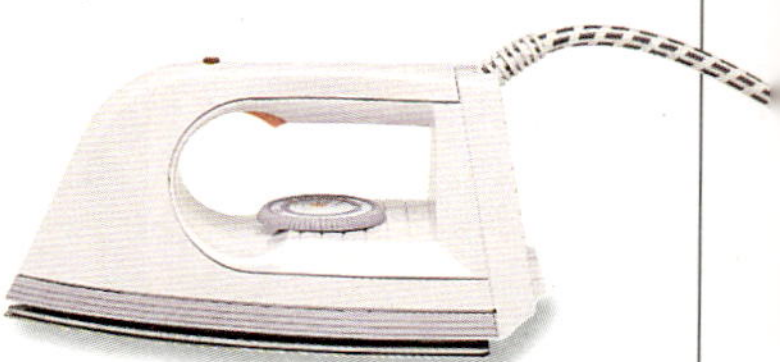

△ ***Iron:** Heat and moisture from the iron, rather than its weight, ensure good flattening of the fabric.*

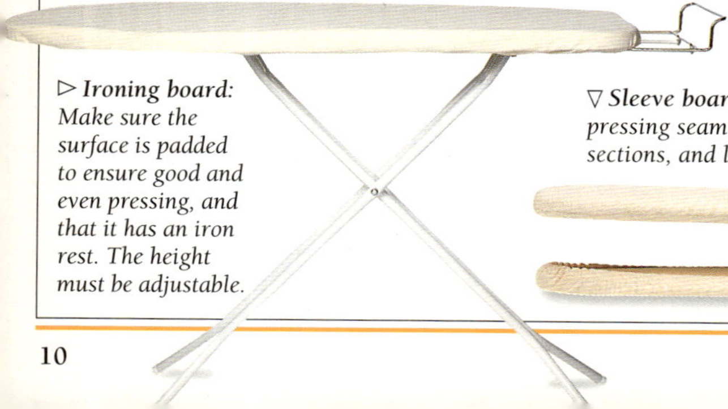

▷ ***Ironing board:** Make sure the surface is padded to ensure good and even pressing, and that it has an iron rest. The height must be adjustable.*

▽ ***Sleeve board:** Useful extra for pressing seams, narrow garment sections, and long, straight seams.*

6 HOW A SEWING MACHINE WORKS

A sewing machine combines two separate threads to make each stitch. The top thread is fed through the fabric by a needle and looped with the bobbin thread to form a stitch. The fabric is guided through the machine by hand, and held firm by a presser foot (*Tip* 23).

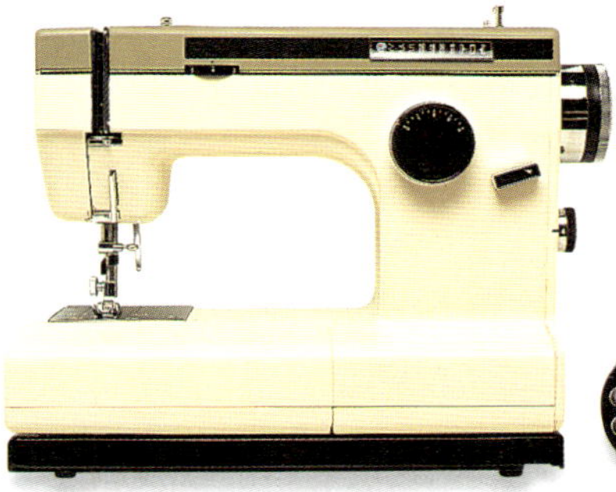

◁ ***Sewing machine*** *needs to have the basic stitches, reverse settings, and sewing attachments. Read the instructions.*

▷ ***Machine foot*** *holds fabric flat and guides the needle smoothly.*

◁ ***Bobbins*** *are wound around with thread.*

7 SEWING MACHINE NEEDLES

Needles come in a range of sizes and point types to work on different thicknesses and weaves of fabric. They should be changed after each item is finished, since blunt needles can mark fabric. The right type of point is vital.

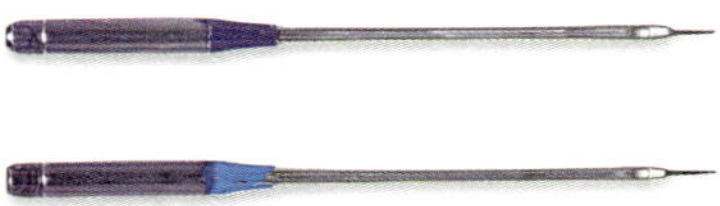

△ ***90/100 machine denim needles*** *are sharp, thick needles that are specifically designed to pierce denim, canvas, and other heavy fabrics.*

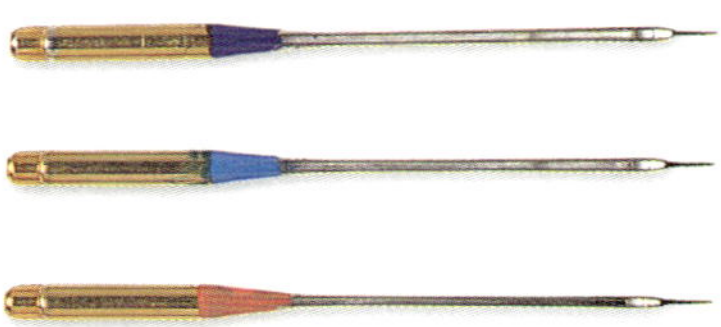

△ ***80/90/100 machine ball-point needles*** *have a round tip and are used when sewing knitwear. The point slides between the yarns instead of piercing them.*

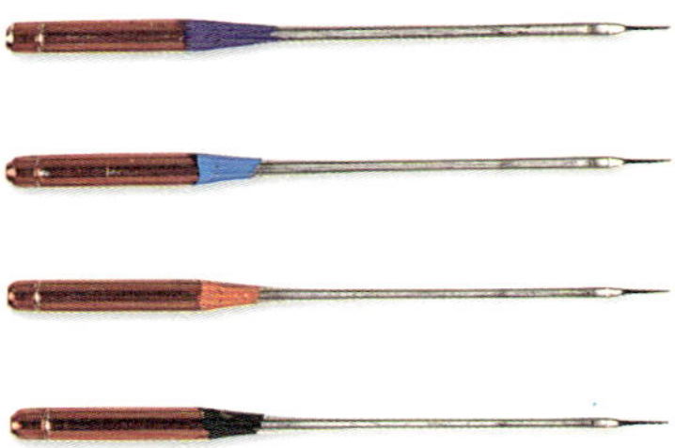

△ ***70/80/90/100 general purpose machine needles*** *are numbered by size, working on the principle of the smaller the number, the finer the needle.*

THREADS & FABRICS

8 TYPES OF THREAD

Select the strength and color of your thread according to the material and color of the fabric. So use cotton thread for cotton and wool or, alternatively, try a multipurpose polyester thread for most fabric types. Use the same threads both for machine and handstitching.

△ ***Basting thread*** *is easily pulled and broken off. This is suitable only for temporary, not permanent, stitching.*

△ ***Cotton thread*** *is ideal for machine- and handstitching on cottons, rayons, and linens.*

△ ***Polyester thread:*** *strong yet elastic thread for synthetic and natural fabrics.*

△ ***Silk thread:*** *A fine thread best used with silk and lightweight fine wools.*

◁ ***Buttonhole twist:*** *A strong, thick silk used for handstitching buttonholes and attaching buttons.*

▷ ***Spooled thread:*** *You can buy all popular threads on spools, which fit over the spool pin on a machine.*

9 COTTON FABRICS

Cotton is soft and comfortable to wear and is perfect for beginners wanting to sew a dress. Start with a light- to mediumweight cotton or cotton blend. Test for crease resistance by crushing a piece of the fabric in one hand. On release, the wrinkles should fall out.

Gingham: *Lightweight and strong fabric with even checks.*

Madras cotton: *Woven in different colors to form patterns. Good for casuals, but creases.*

Chambray: *Easy to sew, light- to mediumweight fabric that wears well. Often used for shirts and children's wear.*

Lawn: *Smooth and absorbent, this lightweight, crisp cotton is good for blouses, soft collars, and sleeve cuffs.*

Poplin: *Versatile and absorbent fabric used mainly for shirts, blouses, and dresses.*

10 WOOLEN FABRICS

A comfortable and versatile fabric, wool absorbs moisture well and is flame resistant, water repellent, and elastic. Be careful when pressing wool; use a damp cloth and press on the wrong side to avoid a shine. Do not slide the iron, since this can stretch the fabric out of shape.

***Worsted:** High-quality, hard-wearing fabric that does not sag.*

***Challis:** Lightweight, soft, easy to handle; often has floral or paisley pattern.*

***Gabardine:** Used mainly for coats, skirts, and pants, this fabric is especially water repellent.*

***Single jersey:** Has vertical ribs on right side, horizontal ribs on wrong side. For casual wear.*

***Lightweight, fine wool:** Crease-resistant wool for full skirts, dresses, and blouses.*

11 LINEN & SILK FABRICS

Linen is cool, highly absorbent, and ideal for hot climates. It is often mixed with other fabrics because it can crease easily. Silk is a high-quality, luxury fabric but it also comes in blends, especially with wool and cotton. Linen-and-silk makes an easy-to-handle mix.

Suiting linen: *Strong and absorbent, with a crisp finish. Good for shirts and skirts.*

Linen-and-silk mix: *Shiny and dense, for skirts and dresses.*

Crêpe-de-chine: *Mediumweight, smooth silk that drapes well. Used for blouses and lingerie.*

Noil: *Raw silk with small cocoon flecks woven into the fibers.*

Shantung: *Mediumweight silk with rough texture, for shirts and dresses.*

12 SYNTHETIC & SPECIAL FABRICS

Polyester, nylon, and acrylic are the best-known synthetics and are durable, hardwearing, and crease resistant, but not absorbent. Rayons, such as viscose, are absorbent but tend to crease and shrink. Use these fabrics when you've gained a little experience.

Crêpon: *Soft, pliable, comfortable, this fabric is often used for blouses.*

Viscose: *Absorbent, soft, and mothproof, it drapes well on skirts and dresses.*

Polyester crêpe: *Crease resistant and hardwearing, this synthetic is used for lingerie, blouses, dresses, and evening wear.*

Microfiber: *Densely woven and durable; usually made from polyester.*

Acetate: *Similar to viscose, this lustrous fabric is good for sportswear.*

BASIC STITCHES

13 SECURING A THREAD

Thread ends need to be firmly secured, whether you are making permanent garment stitches, or stitches to hold fabric together temporarily – as in basting. The knot shown here is for basting, since you can undo it by simply pulling the short end.

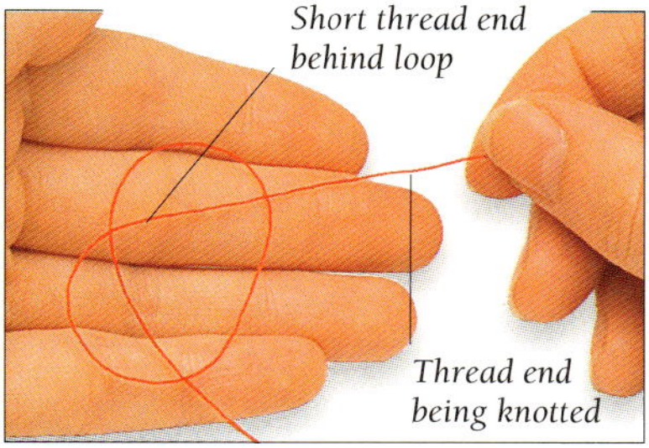

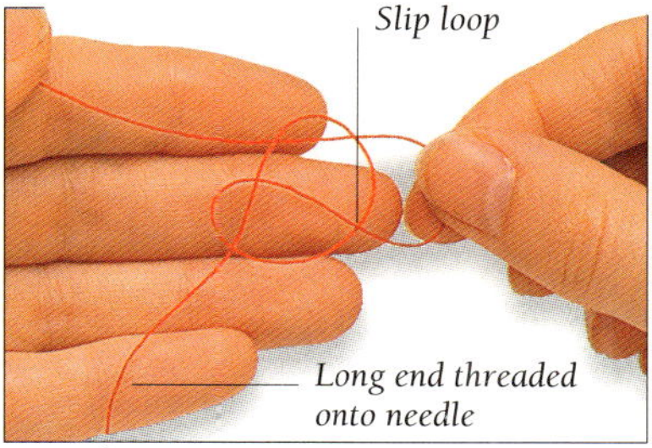

1 Thread a needle, then form a loop near the thread end, passing the short end over the long end and behind the loop. Pull thread through the loop.

2 This forms another loop. Now pull the needle end of the thread until it forms a knot. Try not to pull the short end or to slip the loop through.

14 ROLLING A KNOT

Wrap the thread around one forefinger. Roll the crossed threads between thumb and forefinger. Slip the loop off the finger, pinch it with thumb and forefinger, and pull the other end to tie the knot. Now you can start stitching.

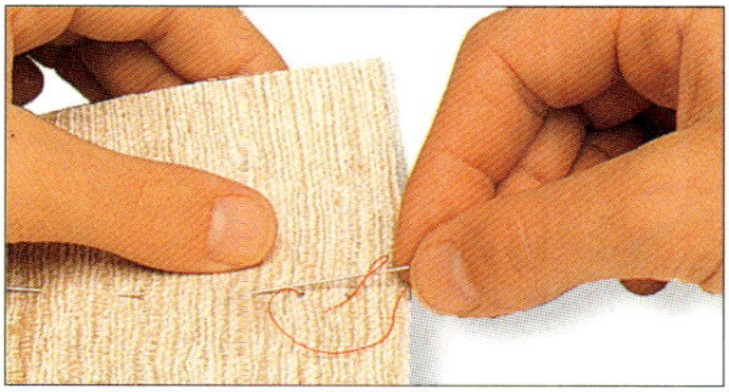

ROLLED KNOT

15 SECURING A THREAD

To begin a permanent stitch or firm basting stitch, use a knot and backstitch. A backstitch helps make strong seams or finishes off a line of stitching (*Tip 20*). A double backstitch gives a firmer and flatter start on permanent stitching than a knot. Work on the wrong side.

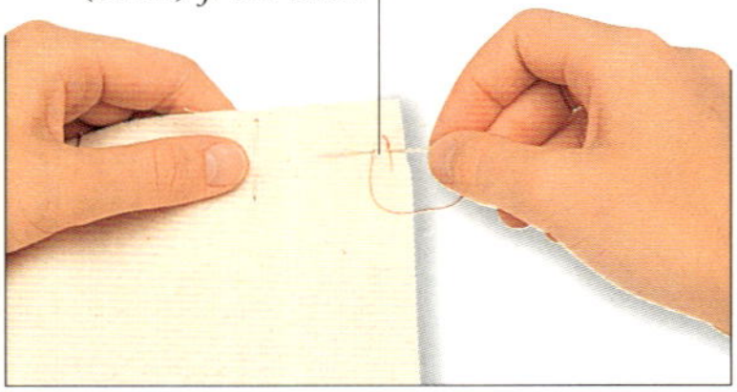

KNOT & BACKSTITCH
Make a knot. Insert the needle, bringing it out close to the knot. Insert the needle again at the knot and make a backstitch.

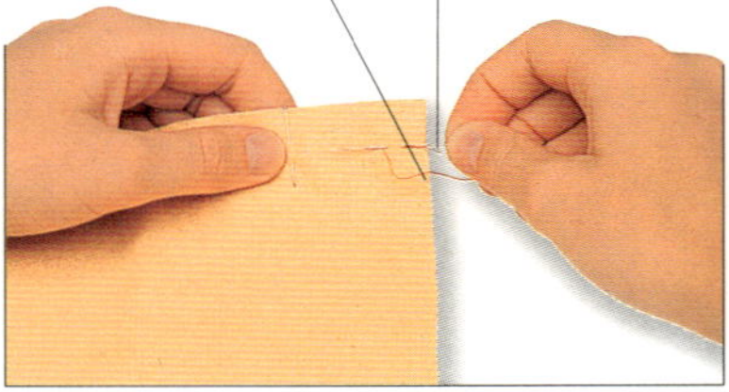

DOUBLE BACKSTITCH
Make a ⅛in (3mm) long stitch; leave a loose end. Make a backstitch in the same place, then a second backstitch over the first.

16 MAKING A RUNNING STITCH

You can work this stitch quickly when seaming or gathering. Work from right to left, taking the needle point in and out of the fabric, and picking up a number of stitches before pulling through.

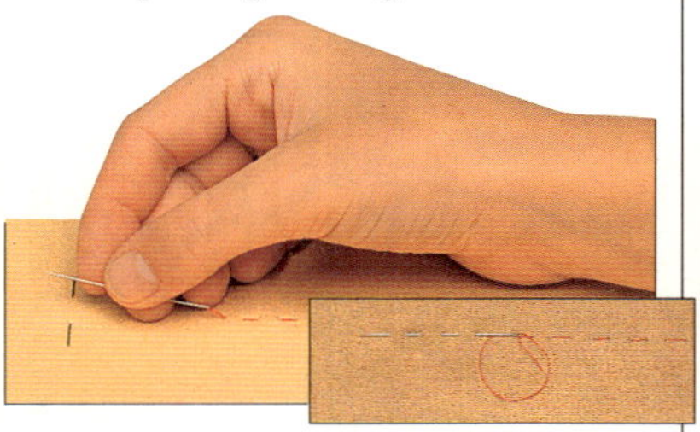

SMALL STITCHES ABOUT ⅛IN (3MM) APART

17 QUICK SLIPSTITCH

To join two folded, abutting edges together, take a ¼in (6mm) stitch through one folded edge (working from right to left). Make a stitch of the same length through the other folded edge. Then continue stitching.

TWO FOLDED EDGES JOINED

18 BASIC & LONG DIAGONAL BASTING

Basting holds fabric together temporarily but securely before you make a permanent stitch. Use a different color thread for basting so you can easily distinguish it from the permanent thread when removing it. Avoid using inexpensive basting thread, since the dye may not be colorfast and strong color can mark light fabric.

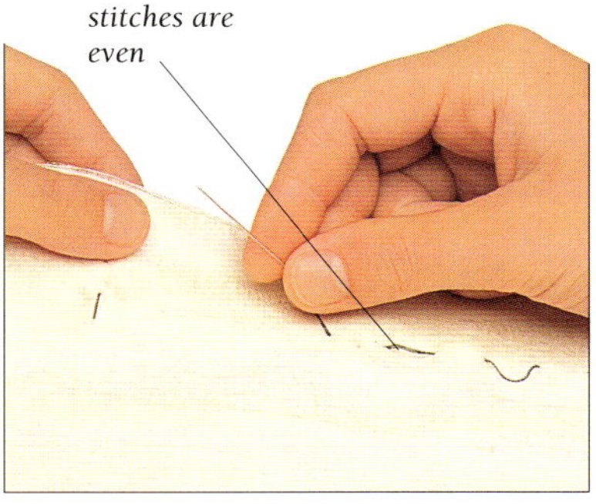

△ BASIC BASTING
Insert the needle into the wrong side. Work from left to right, bringing the needle in and out about ¼–⅜in (6–10mm) apart. Ensure these large stitches are of equal length on both sides of the fabric.

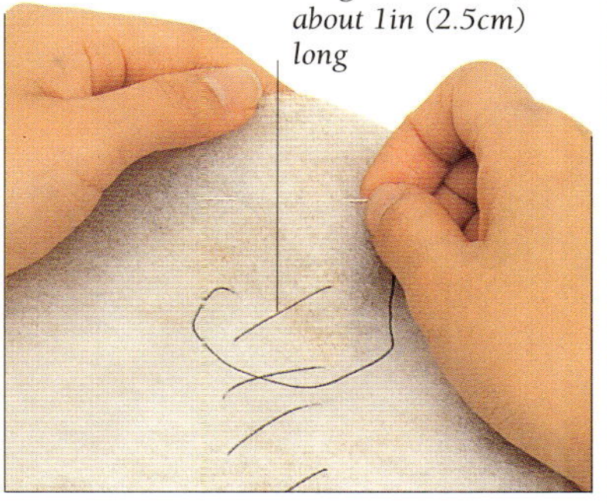

△ LONG DIAGONAL BASTING
This is used to hold two layers of fabric together over a large area. Take a stitch about 1in (2.5cm) long, then move up, and make another stitch to form a long diagonal stitch. Repeat.

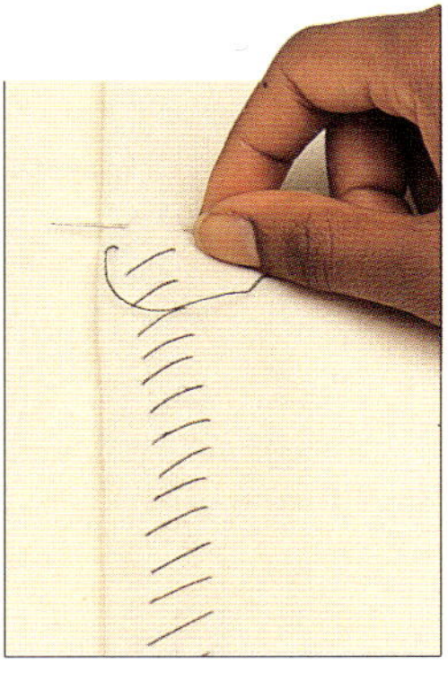

◁ SHORT DIAGONAL BASTING
Use the same method as for long diagonal tacking (above), but with shorter, closer-together stitches. This is a fast way to hold several fabric layers together, as in a pleat (Tip 53).

WHEN TO USE HANDSTITCHING
Despite the ease and help of modern machines in most areas of stitching, you still need to be able to handle a needle and thread with confidence. Handstitches give a superior quality finish in most stages of garment making, from transferring pattern markings with tailor's tacks (Tip 33) *to stitching the final hem* (Tip 63). *When handstitching, try to keep the stitches neat and even.*

19 Overcast stitch

Also known as an overedge stitch, this is handy for finishing raw edges. Take the needle through the fabric, working from back to front, ⅛in (2–3mm) from the raw edge. Move the needle along to the left and bring it out again through the fabric from back to front. Continue sewing like this.

STITCHES SLANTED & EVENLY SPACED

20 Backstitching a seam

A strong stitch for seaming, you could also use this instead of a machine straight stitch on small areas. Take a small stitch, working from right to left. Insert the needle at the start of the previous stitch, and bring it out beyond the point where the thread emerges.

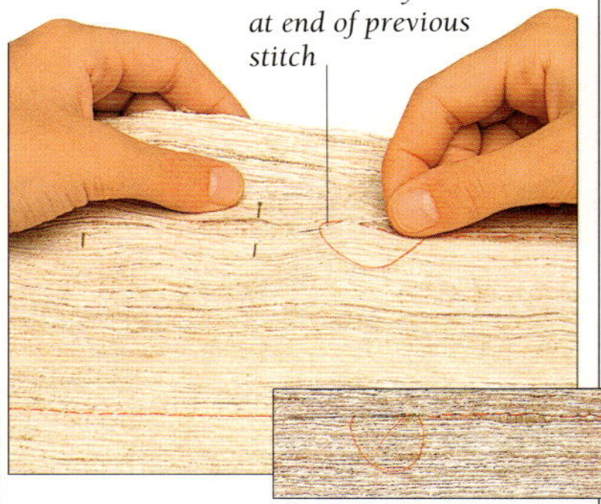

STITCHES LOOK LIKE MACHINE STITCHES

21 Finishing off

The best way to ensure a really durable finish to permanent stitching is by taking a small backstitch (*Tip 20*) over a few threads and leaving a small loop. Make another stitch in the same place, and pass the needle through the loop of the first stitch. Pull the thread secure. Make the securing stitches as small as possible, and work on the fabric's wrong side.

22 WORKING MACHINE STITCHES

Before trying decorative stitches, learn first how to make functional machine stitches to construct a garment – like the two essential ones shown below. The number of different stitches a sewing machine produces varies with each make. When buying your model (*Tip 6*), make sure it has the stitches you need.

△ STRAIGHT STITCH
Start 3/8–5/8in (1–1.5cm) from fabric edge. Reverse stitch to edge. Stitch forward on top of this, then reverse stitch to finish.

△ ZIGZAG STITCH
To finish raw edges and for buttonholes, stitch on edge so outer swing of stitch falls outside raw edge. Use medium settings.

23 MACHINE THREAD TENSION

The machine bobbin (*Tip 6*) needs to be wound evenly. Then, with needle threaded, raise it to expose the eye with the guide at its highest position. Turn the hand-wheel until the needle enters the bobbin case and then returns to its highest position. As it rises, it pulls up a loop of bobbin thread. Pull loop to bring bobbin thread through.

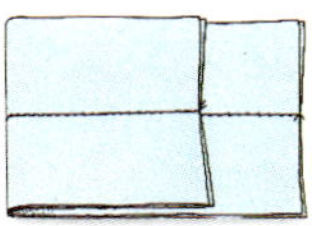

CORRECT TENSION

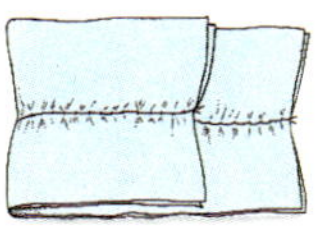

TOP THREAD TOO TIGHT

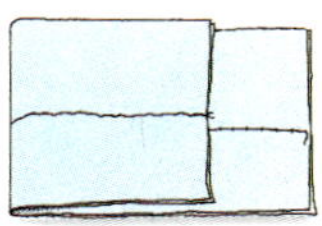

TOP THREAD TOO LOOSE

◁ ***Tension controls** for needle and bobbin threads must balance to draw both threads evenly into the fabric.*

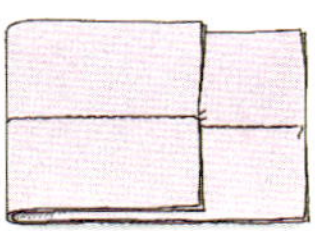

CORRECT PRESSURE

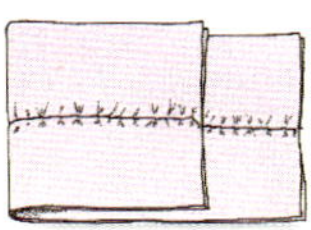

TOO MUCH PRESSURE

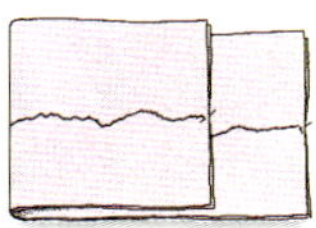

TOO LITTLE PRESSURE

◁ ***Presser foot** exerts downward pressure; feed teeth, upward force. Both work to make even stitches.*

Working with a Pattern

24 Choosing a Pattern Size

Compare your own measurements to those of the pattern. The pattern allows for ease between body size and pattern piece size. To check height, stand by a wall with a ruler flat on head; mark wall with pencil. Measure from mark to floor.

△ *Pattern pieces are measured between seamlines, not from edge to edge. Patterns include tolerance, which is the extra size needed to give room.*

▷ ***Measurements** for bust, waist, hips, height, and back-of-neck-to-waist are needed for a perfect fit.*

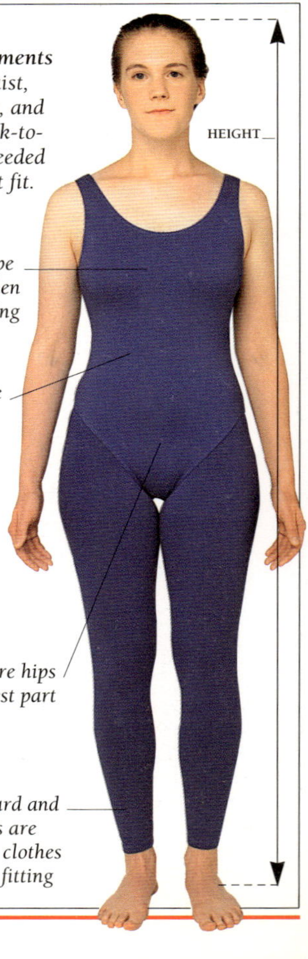

25 TAKING VITAL MEASUREMENTS

Before buying a pattern, take at least four accurate body measurements. Ask a friend to help and have the tape measure (*Tip 2*) kept taut at all times. Underwear is fine if you have no close-fitting garment to wear. Your body size is unlikely to match the pattern size exactly, so choose a size that comes closest to your largest measurement.

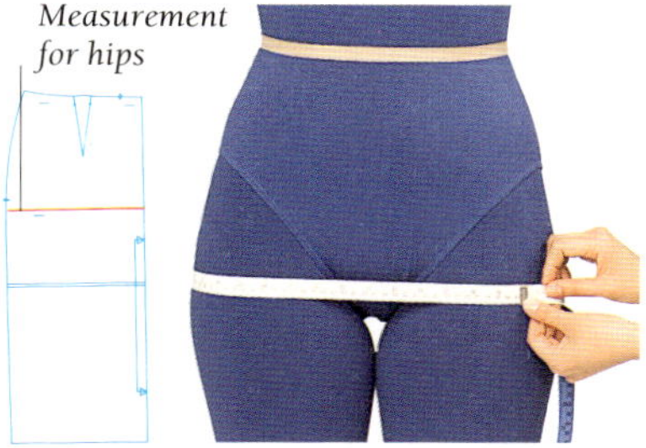

△ **Hips**: *measure around the fullest part of the hips, about 7–9in (18–23cm) below the waist. This will vary according to your height. Choose a pattern for a skirt by hip rather than waist size. The pattern will allow for ease.*

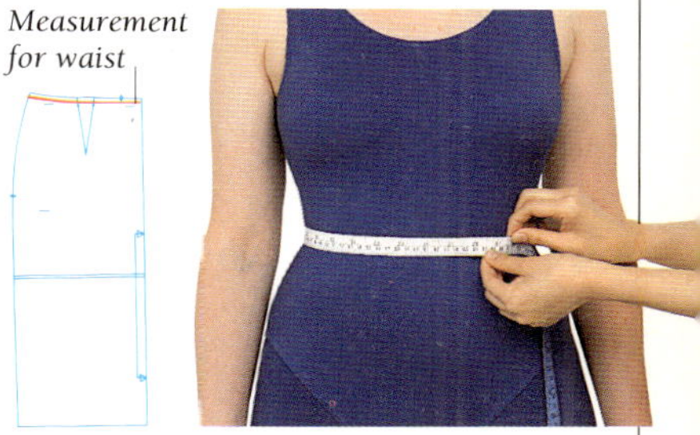

△ **Waist**: *use a ribbon or string, and tie it loosely around the waist. Adjust it so it settles into your natural waistline. Now measure around this marker with a tape measure* (Tip 2). *In this instance, do not pull the tape measure tight.*

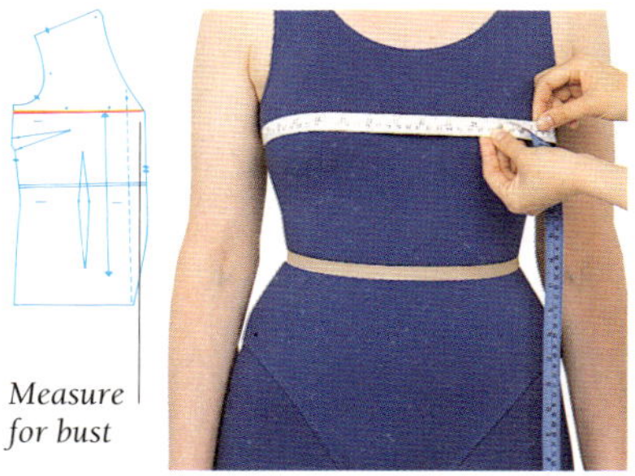

△ **Bust**: *measure around the fullest part of the bust and the widest part of the back, keeping the tape measure reasonably taut. You'll need a friend to help you hold this straight around your back. For a pattern for a top only, go by the bust size.*

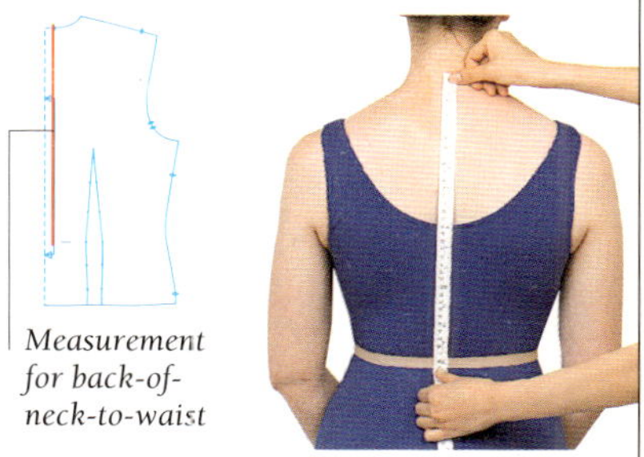

△ **Back-of-neck-to-waist**: *with a friend to help you measure where you cannot reach, measure from the protruding vertebra at the neck base to the waistline marker. This measurement should be compared with the pattern piece for fit.*

26 READING A PATTERN

The envelope front (*Tip 24*) shows the finished garment, while the back details the fabric amount needed for each view. Size charts, recommended fabrics, and drawings of the garment details are also given. Inside is an instruction sheet and the pattern tissue.

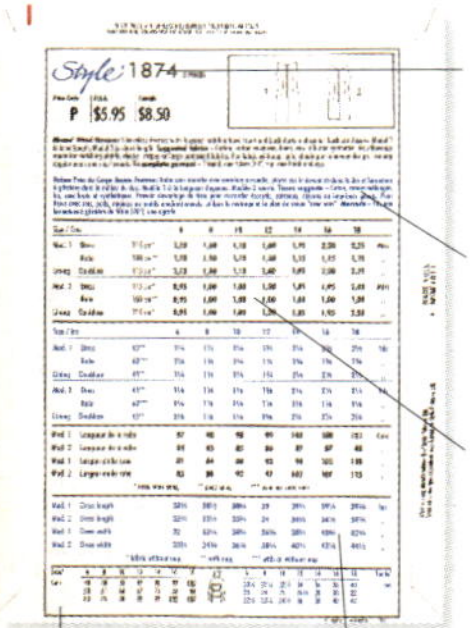

27 MULTISIZE ALTERATIONS

When ready to cut out, remove the pattern tissue from the envelope, open out the sheets, and smooth out.

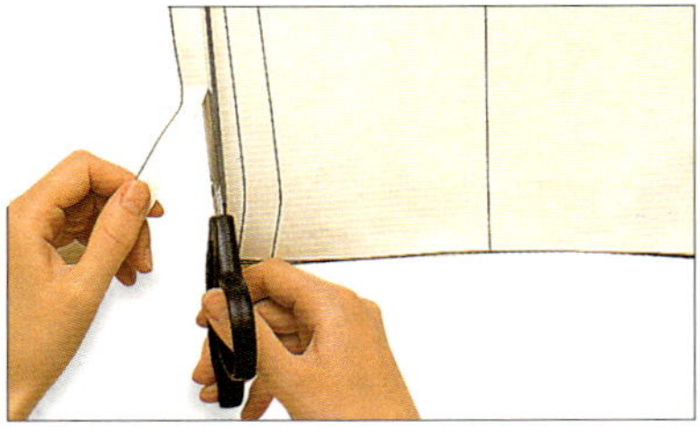

1 △ For body measurements between sizes, cut the pattern between the two size lines. Ensure you cut evenly and accurately between the lines.

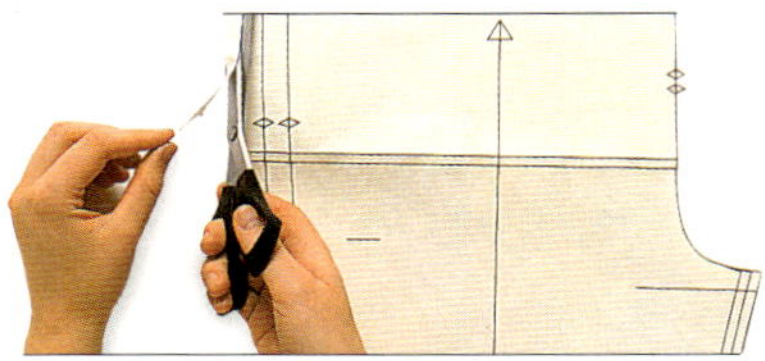

2 △ For individual pattern adjustments, say for large hips and a small waist, cut to the hips on the larger size. Taper to the next size down at the waist.

28 FABRIC GRAIN

Warp, or lengthwise, threads run parallel to selvages (the finished edges on woven fabrics); weft, or crosswise, threads weave across. Warp grain is less likely to stretch and is usually used as the straight grain.

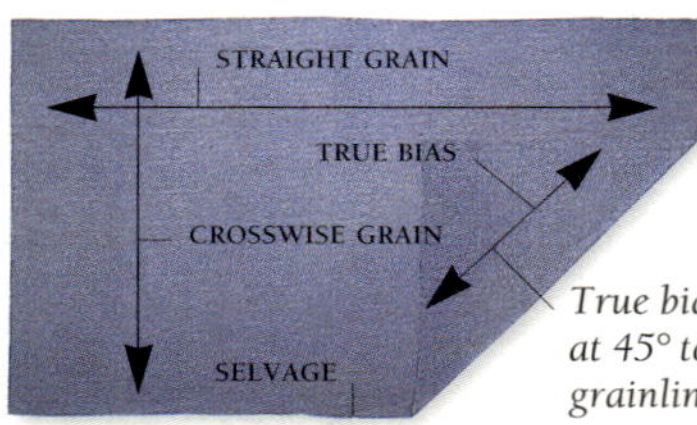

29 PREPARING PATTERN PIECES

Choose and separate the pieces before cutting out. Make sure you smooth out the tissue, since the pieces will be a distorted shape if it is creased. Use a warm iron to flatten the tissue, if need be.

1 △ Find the drawings of the pattern pieces on the instruction leaflet. Identify and mark the required pieces.

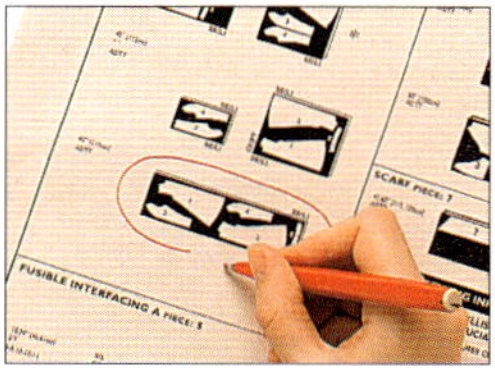

2 △ Select the cutting layouts on the leaflet. Circle the correct layout for garment view, size, and fabric width.

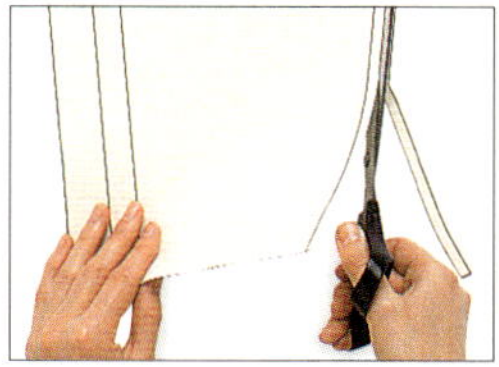

3 △ Cut out the pieces from the pattern tissue. Cut multisize pieces accurately to the chosen size.

30 LAYING OUT A PATTERN

Pattern pieces normally represent a garment's right half. When positioning with straight arrows, keep arrows parallel to finished edge, so fabric is straight when cut. Pieces with bent arrows are cut with the edge to which the arrows point on the fabric fold.

31 PINNING PATTERN TO FABRIC

Before you pin, fold the fabric in half lengthwise with right sides together. A pattern piece has a straight grain arrow (which must be placed parallel to the edge or fold) or a bent arrow. Check alignments.

Pins spaced about 4in (10cm) apart on straight edges, closer on curves

Tape measure

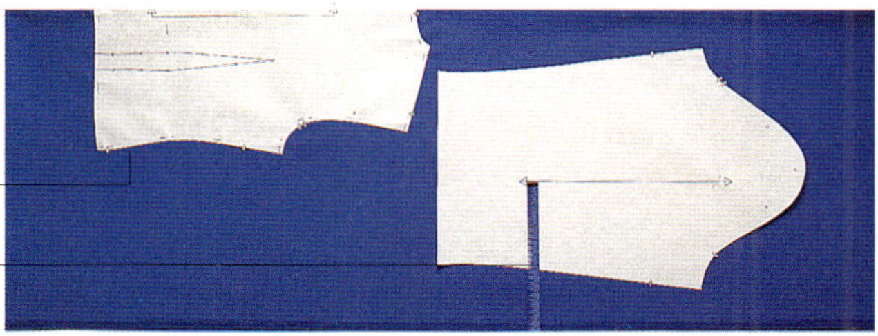

32 CUTTING OUT PATTERN PIECES

Slide the scissors along the fabric, making long cuts on the straight edges and shorter cuts at the curves. Try always to cut smoothly, and avoid making jagged edges. Be sure to use a sharp pair of sewing scissors (*Tip 1*): blunt ones make the edges look ragged. Place one hand lightly on the pattern piece, and cut with the other hand.

△ CUTTING METHOD
Rest the scissors on the table with the fabric slightly raised for a smooth cut.

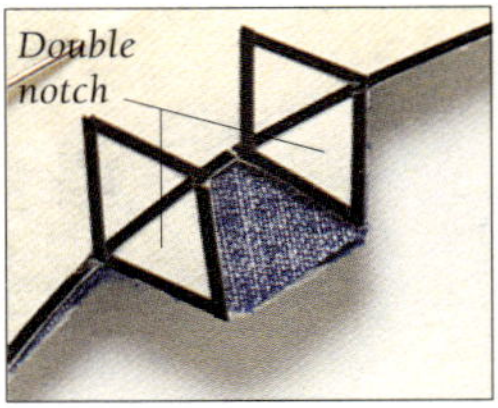

△ NOTCHES
Cut across double notch markings from point to point, not around each notch.

33 MAKING TAILOR'S TACKS

These are made with doubled thread in contrasting color. Use single tailor's tacks to mark circles, dots, buttonhole ends, and other pattern markings on a double or single layer.

CONTINUOUS TACKS
Show pattern line markings such as center front line or pleat foldline with continuous tacks.

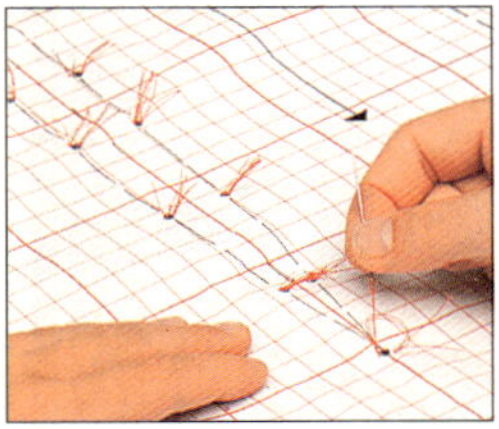

1 Stitch through the pattern and both fabric layers. Leave ⅝in (1.5cm) thread ends. Repeat with a 1¼in (3cm) loop.

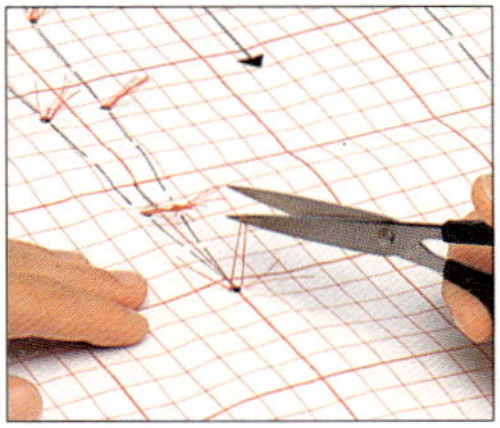

2 Check stitching has gone through bottom layer. Snip thread leaving ⅝in (1.5cm) thread ends. Cut thread at loop center.

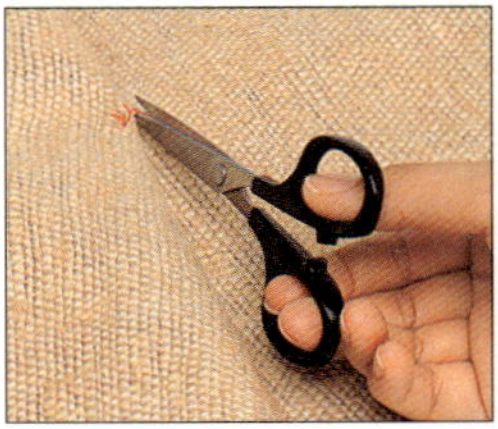

3 Pull pattern away and separate fabric layers so you can clearly see tacks. Snip tacks between layers, leaving tufts.

WORKING WITH SEAMS

34 USING SEAM GUIDES

To make a seam, two or more pieces of fabric are joined together – usually with a line of machine stitching. In order to keep the stitching evenly spaced, you need to use the seam guidelines on your sewing machine, or you can use a seam gauge that is fixed to the needle plate and forms a guide for sewing straight seams.

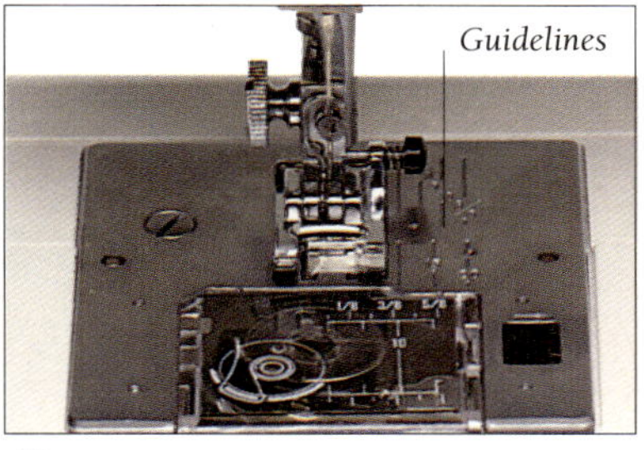

1 △ Check the plate beneath the foot of your machine. It will have a central hole for the needle and etched lines for the seam guides.

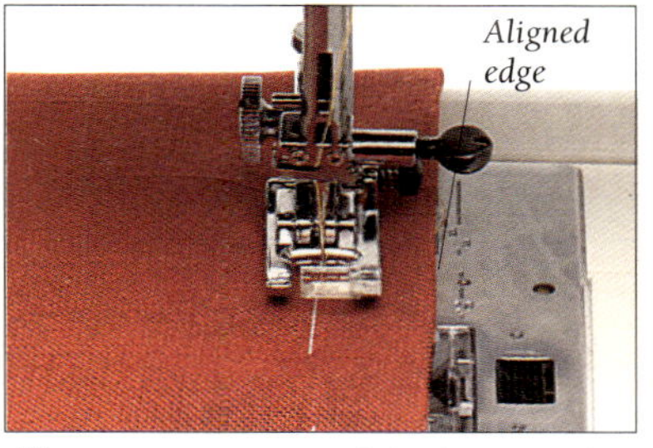

2 △ Align the edge of the fabric with the correct guideline. Keep parallel to this line during stitching. To ensure straight seams, practice on spare fabric.

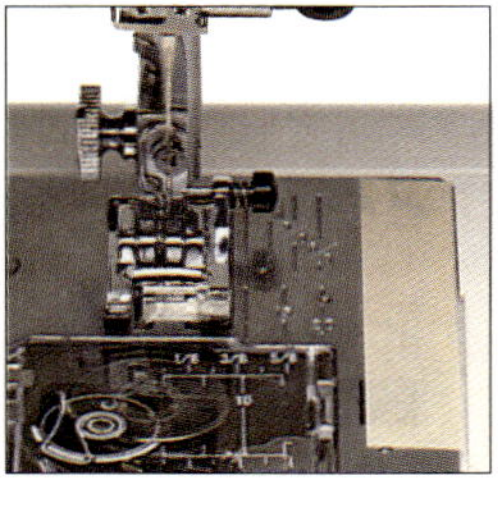

◁ MASKING TAPE GUIDE

If you require an unusual seam width, use a tape measure and masking tape to mark where to align the edge of the fabric. For accurate stitching of corners, also stick tape in front of the foot at a right angle from the needle.

SEAM TYPES

The plain, or flat, seam that joins the edges of two pieces of fabric is suitable for most fabrics. French seams (Tip 40) conceal all raw edges and are ideal for fine fabrics or those that fray easily.

35 MAKING A PLAIN SEAM

The most basic and easiest seam to make, a plain seam is suitable for many different styles of garment. To ensure absolutely straight edges, it is best to practice stitching while keeping the fabric edge aligned with the seam guideline. Begin by placing the fabric edges together with right sides facing and raw edges even.

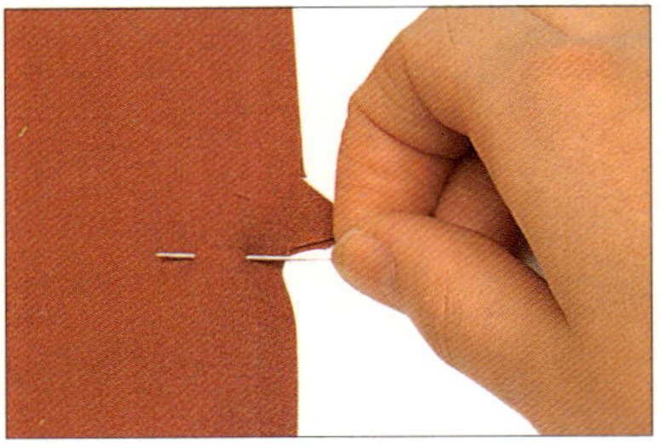

1 △ Pin the seam edges together through the wrong side of the fabric so that the pins are placed at a right angle to the seamline.

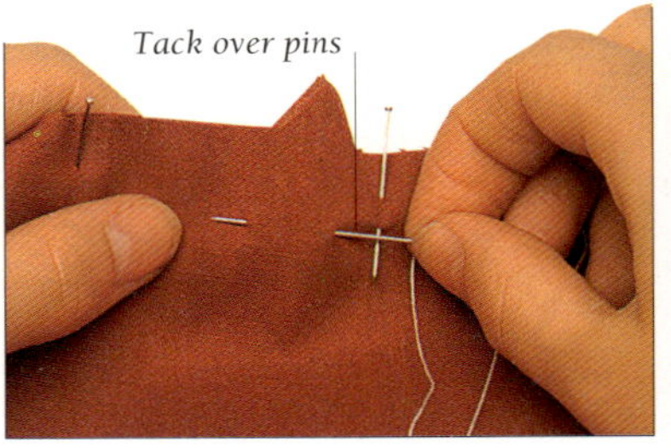

2 △ Baste the pinned seam close to the seamline. A seam allowance is normally ⅝in (1.5cm), so baste just short of this distance from the edge.

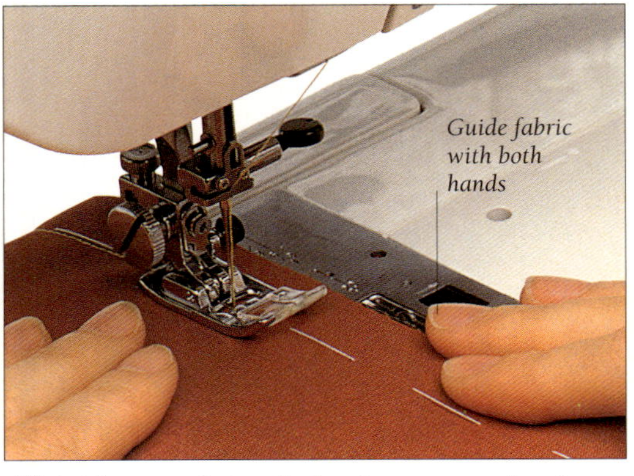

3 △ After completing the basting, remove the pins. Position the needle on the seamline ⅝in (1.5cm) from the edge. Reverse stitch to the edge, then stitch forward along the seamline.

4 △ Reverse stitch to finish the seam. Remove all basting. Open all seam allowances and press flat. Neaten the raw edge, if needed, to prevent fraying, using a seam finish (*Tip 39*).

36 STITCHING A CORNER

To stitch corners or curves as for collars or cuffs, or to add neat detailing to topstitching, you will need to pivot the fabric with the needle down. The trick is to pivot accurately exactly at the corner, and mark the corner point with a crosswise pin or basting.

1 ▷ Use the seam guide to get an even seam, and stitch toward the corner ⅝in (1.5cm) from the edge. Stop ⅝in (1.5cm) short of the end. Check that the needle is lowered in the fabric.

2 △ Now lift the presser foot and pivot the fabric around the needle, so that the second edge lies parallel to the ⅝in (1.5cm) seam guideline on the sewing machine needle plate.

3 △ Lower the foot and continue to stitch, again keeping the edge of the fabric aligned with the ⅝in (1.5cm) seam guideline. Continue sewing in this way until the end of the seam.

37 REDUCING SEAM BULK

Seam allowances are the amount of fabric allowed for on a pattern where sections of an item are to be joined together by a seam. Trim seam allowances that are enclosed within a finished part of the garment to reduce their bulk. You will also need to clip or notch the trimmed seam allowance for curved seams so they will lie flat.

△ TRIMMING
Trim both seam allowances together to about half the original seam width before pressing. This is usually sufficient for seams on light- to mediumweight fabrics.

△ CLIPPING
Inward curved seams (as on collars) need clipping. Cut into the seam allowances up to the stitching to allow the fabric to open out, and to fit around the curve.

▽ NOTCHING
To form a notch – which is a small, V-shaped wedge cut out of the seam allowance on outward curves – first cut one side of the V-shape, then cut the other side.

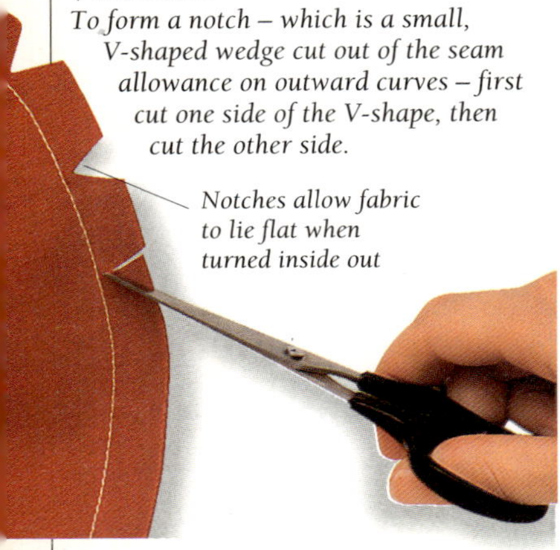

△ CLIPPING & NOTCHING
Where an inward curve is stitched to an outward curve, clip one seam allowance so that the edge lies flat, and notch the other to remove excess fullness.

38 TRIMMING A POINT

On corners where the seams are stitched along both sides, it is important to trim the seam allowances well in order to achieve a sharp point when the corner is turned right side out.

1 Trim across the point just a few threads outside the seam stitching. The sharper the point, the closer to the stitching the trimming must be.

2 Trim both seam allowances at an angle toward the corner point. When turned right side out, allowance should sit neatly inside the point.

39 WORKING SEAM FINISHES

Seam finishes neaten seam allowances and protect seams from wear and tear. Zigzag stitch is the most widely used finish for seams, although the type of finish depends on the fabric and if the seam shows.

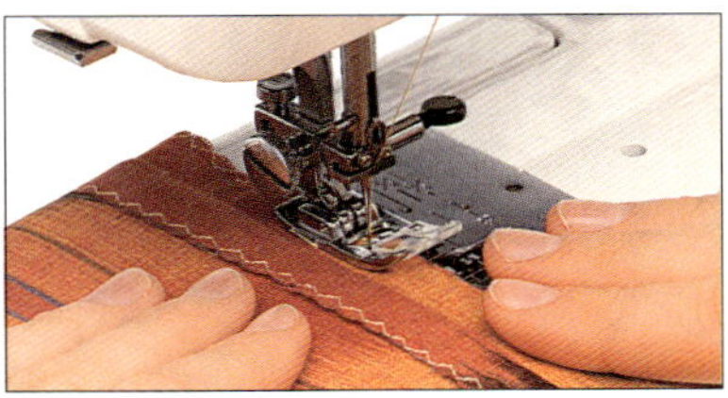

△ ZIGZAG-STITCHED
Work on seam allowance edges with medium-length stitch on light/medium fabrics.

△ TURNED & STITCHED
For cottons, fold ⅛in (3mm) to the wrong side along each raw edge. Stitch along fold.

◁ TRIMMED & ZIGZAGGED
If seam shows, trim to half original width, zigzag stitch edges and press for neat finish.

▷ PINKED
Trim close to fabric edges using pinking shears.

40 Making a French Seam

A self-enclosed seam, a French seam is neat, narrow, and perfect for sheer fabrics where the seam allowances are visible, since it conceals all raw edges. However, it should be used only on straight fabric edges. This type of seam is machine stitched, and when finished should be no more than about ¼in (6mm) in width. Place the fabric with the wrong sides together and raw edges even.

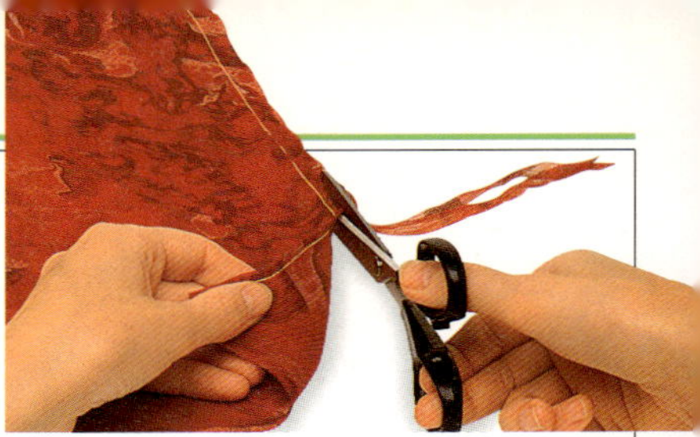

1 △ Pin close to the seamline and then stitch the two pieces of fabric together, making a seam ⅜in (1cm) in from the fabric edge. Now trim both seam allowances to ⅛in (3mm).

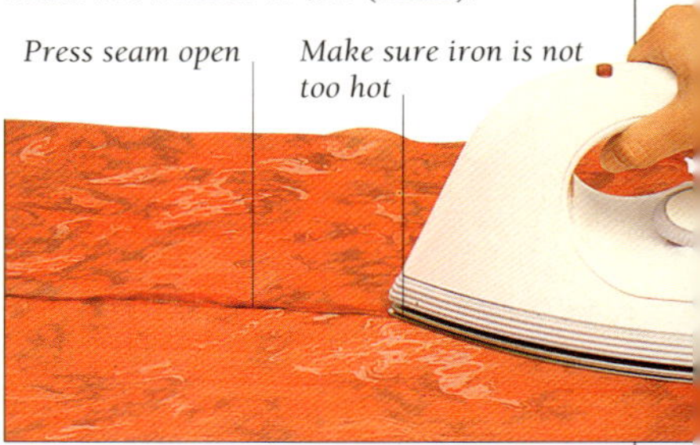

Press seam open

Make sure iron is not too hot

2 ▷ Press the seam open. Fold the right sides together and position the seam centrally along the fold. Re-press the fabric. If the iron is too hot, this will crease sheer fabric, so test the iron first.

3 △ Baste the two layers of fabric together, stitching close to the ridge formed by the raw edges. Then, on the wrong side of the fabric, stitch ¼in (5mm) in from the folded edge. Press the seam to one side.

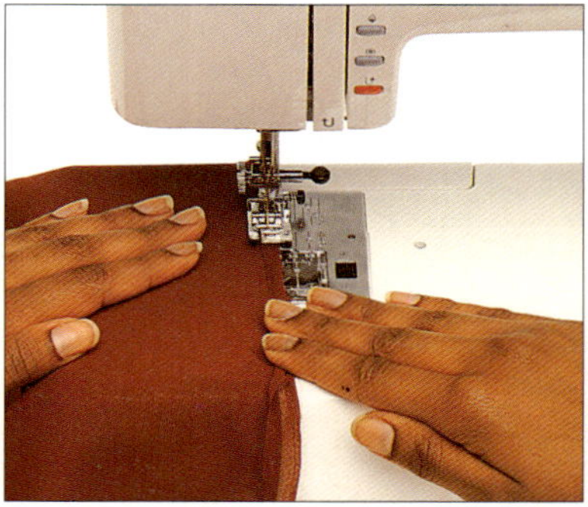

△ Mock French Seam

Use these for curves. Stitch a plain seam (Tip 35). Trim seam allowances to ⅜in (1cm). Fold in ¼in (6mm) along both seam allowances. Press together the folded edges. Stitch allowances along pressed edges.

41 STITCHING CURVED SEAMS

A curved (also called a Princess) seam is formed by joining inward and outward curves. The curved seam is shaped out over the bust, fitted at the waist, and shaped out toward the hips. You will need to staystitch, which is simply straight machine stitching worked just inside a seam allowance, to add strength and prevent stretching.

1 △ You are likely to have a center panel and two side panels. Staystitch the center panel, just inside the seam from top notch to below second notch under the bust shaping. Clip inward curve.

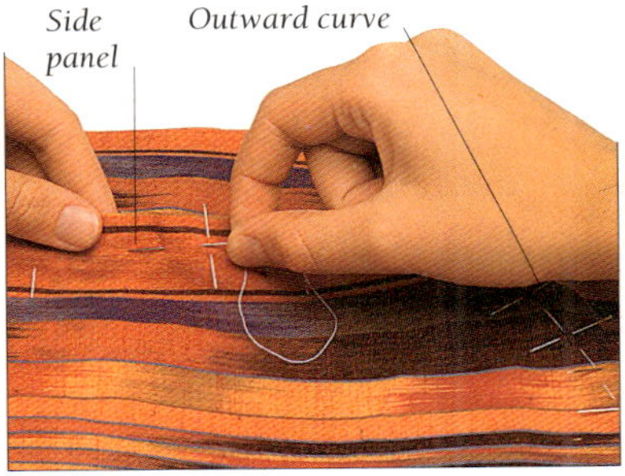

2 △ With right sides together, match the side and center panel with side panel uppermost. Pin the seam, opening up the clips on the center panel to fit around the side panel shaping. Baste.

3 △ Remove the pins and stitch the seam, working with the center panel uppermost. Stitch slowly at the bust shaping, and stop with the needle down to check that the underside is flat.

4 △ Remove basting and open out seam. Cut out small notches from the side panel seam allowance so the panel lies flat. Stagger notches between the clips already on the center panel seam allowance.

TAKING IN FABRIC FULLNESS

42 TYPES OF DARTS

Darts are used mainly on women's clothing to shape fabric around the body's contours and allow for fullness at bust and hips. The wide base of a dart takes in fabric fullness so a garment fits the narrower parts of the body. Small darts can be used to shape elbows and the back of shoulders on tailored garments.

△ ***Waist darts** are plain darts (Tip 43) that shape the fabric in at the waist and give fullness at the hips. There are usually two at the garment front and two or four at the back.*

△ ***Bust darts** add fullness at the bust. The most common type are single bust darts, which start at the underarm side seams.*

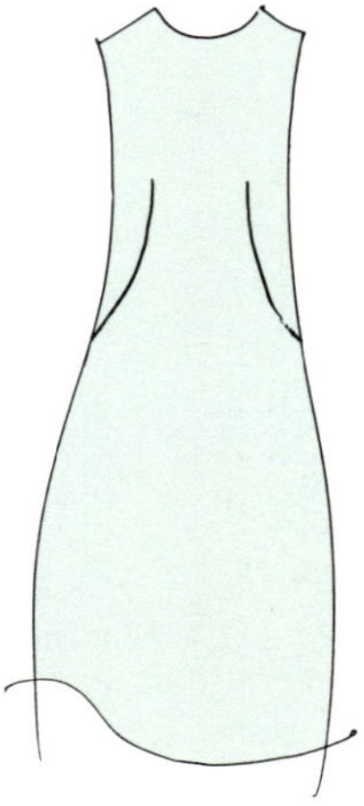

△ ***French darts** are much wider than plain darts, and appear only on the front of garments. They extend from hip or waist level at the side seam to the bust.*

43 MAKING A PLAIN DART

A plain dart is a fold of fabric stitched with a tapering seam to form a fine point. It is made on the wrong side of the garment. The dart is shown on the pattern as a triangle with a central foldline and two stitching lines. You can make slight fit alterations by redrawing dart stitching lines, but do this also on the pattern piece.

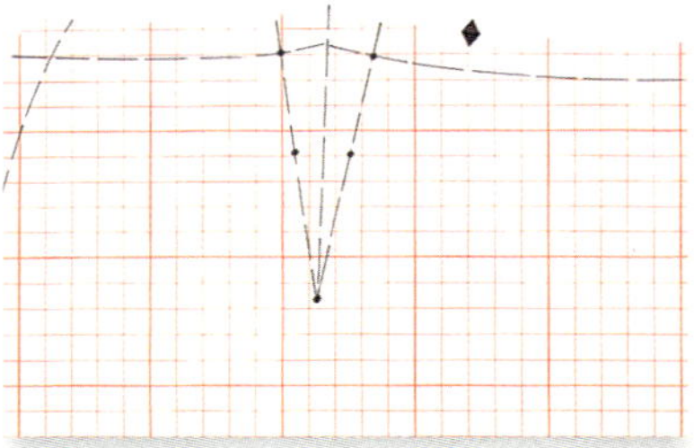

1 △ Check the dart markings are clearly visible on the pattern. Pin the pattern to the fabric. Use tailor's tacks (*Tip 33*) to transfer the dart markings to the fabric.

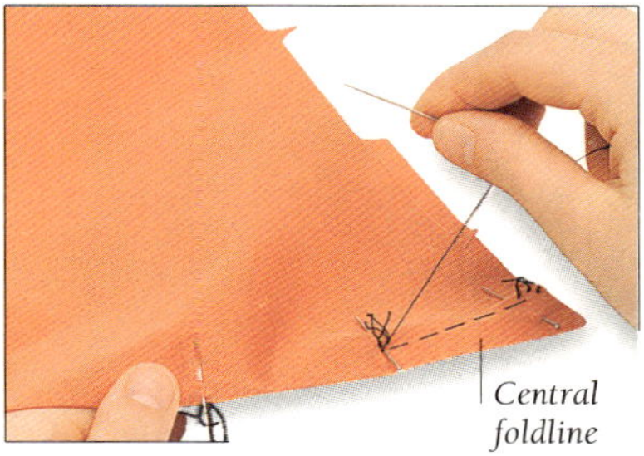

2 △ After removing the pattern from the fabric, work from the wrong side of the fabric. Fold the fabric right sides together along the central foldline, matching the tailor's tacks. Pin and baste.

3 △ Stitch the dart line, starting from the outer edges. Taper gently to the point. Finish with a few backstitches just inside the stitching. Press as stitched to embed the stitching. Then open fabric out flat and press dart to one side.

44 MAKING A DART ON THICK FABRIC

Cut along the fold to ⅝in (1.5cm) from the dart point. Open fabric. Then press dart open toward the point. Press the last 1⅝in (1.5cm) and flatten this over the stitching.

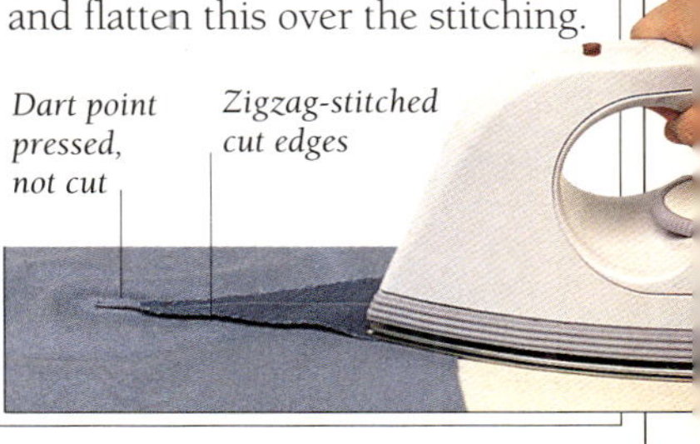

45 MAKING A FRENCH DART

Appearing only on the front of a garment, a French dart extends from hip or waist level at the side seam to the bust. Since it is much wider than a plain dart, a French dart must be cut, or "slashed," to open up the center before it is stitched, so that the stitching lines will align and match perfectly.

ZIGZAG FOR FINISH
Zigzag stitching finishes raw edges on each side of the dart. Adjust settings to medium width and length. Stitch so the outer swing of the stitch falls outside the raw edge.

1 △ Use tailor's tacks (*Tip 33*) to transfer pattern markings, stitching lines, and any fabric central-slash line. Here, the center of the French dart has been cut away, so there is no slash line.

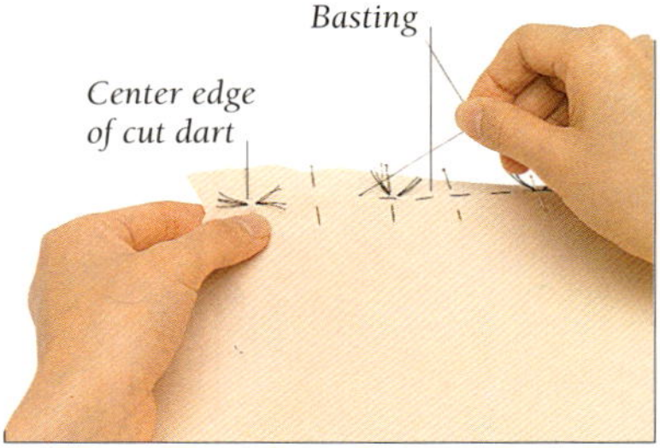

2 △ Remove pattern. Match stitching lines with right sides together, gently easing or stretching if necessary. Pin and baste just inside the stitching line. Check fit. Remove tailor's tacks.

3 △ Stitch along the dart from the outer edge of the fabric piece to the end of the tapered point. Backstitch at each end to finish off the dart and to secure the stitching firmly.

4 △ Remove all basting stitches and finish by using zigzag stitches (*see box above*) along the raw edge. Press the dart as stitched, then open out the fabric and press again.

46 PIN TUCKS

A pin tuck is one of several decorative tucks that add detail and give shape to a garment, and are very easy to make. It is very narrow, being usually only ⅛in (3mm) wide. Pin tucks can be either spaced or blind – that is, having no visible space where the tucks meet.

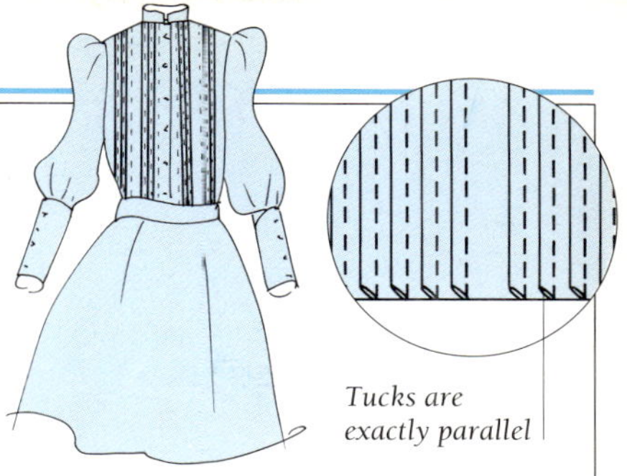

PIN-TUCKED DRESS BODICE

47 MAKING BASIC TUCKS

Tucks are formed by stitching folds of fabric along a straight grain (*Tip 28*). The width and spacing of tucks depends on fabric thickness and the desired decorative detail. To form a tuck, stitch together two stitching lines to create a fold. Form tucks on the right side for decorative effect; for shaping, form them only on the wrong side.

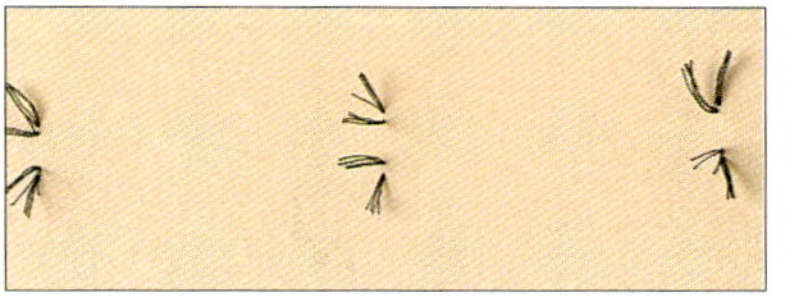

1 △ Mark the stitching lines of the first tuck, using rows of tailor's tacks (*Tip 33*). Mark on the fabric's right side for decorative tucks (on the wrong side for shaping tucks). Clip tailor's tacks and carefully remove the paper pattern.

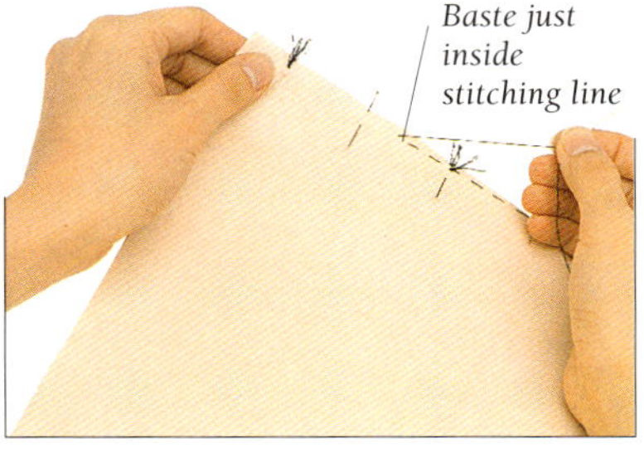

2 △ To bring together the stitching lines, fold the tuck along the center. The distance between stitching lines is twice the finished tuck width. Pin and baste. Remove the tailor's tacks.

3 △ Machine stitch one tuck at a time to create parallel tucks. Cut a strip of cardboard to the tuck width (mark with a notch), plus distance between tucks. Use strip to mark each tuck position.

48 Stitching & Pressing Tucks

The simplest way to stitch neat, parallel folds of fabric is to use the edge of the machine foot as a guide to keep the stitching straight and even. Finish by ironing over with a pressing cloth to press all the tucks flat in the required direction.

▷ Stitching
An alternative to the machine foot for stitching neat tucks is to use markings on the throat plate as a guide. You will need an adjustable sewing-machine attachment, called a seam gauge, to make wide tucks.

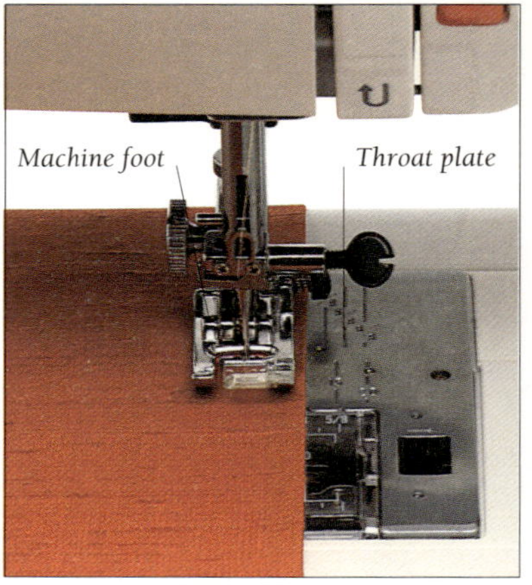

△ Pressing
As you stitch each tuck, press it, using a clean cloth placed over the fabric to prevent marking when pressing. Open out the fabric, and press all the tucks flat.

△ Staystitching
Use staystitches across the ends of the finished tucks to strengthen the seam allowance. This keeps the tucks in place while completing the garment.

49 Using Simple Gathers

Simple gathers are used to draw in fabric for fit. Depending on the fabric weight, the gathers should be two or three times the desired finish length. Adjust the machine stitch to its longest length; loosen tension. Stitch both rows on the same side of the fabric, within the seam allowance. Pull up threads on the wrong side.

50 MAKING & FITTING GATHERS

Gathering stitches are longer than ordinary stitches, and you need to stitch two rows to enable the gathers to form evenly and hang well. Since fabric hangs better with the straight grain (*Tip 28*), make the gathering stitches across the grain. If required, seam the fabric pieces together before starting to gather the edge.

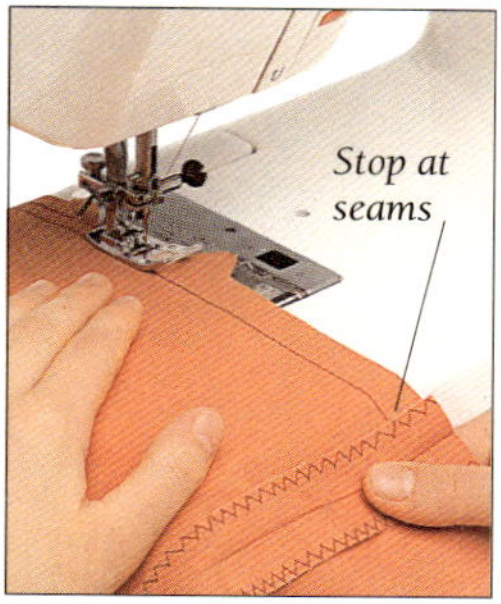

1 △ Stitch two parallel rows ¼in (6mm) apart. Stop at each vertical seam so that seam allowances are not gathered.

2 △ Lay the pieces together with right sides together and raw edges even, and pin at the seams and notches.

3 △ Wind the two gathering threads at one end into a figure-eight around a pin. Ease gathers along the threads.

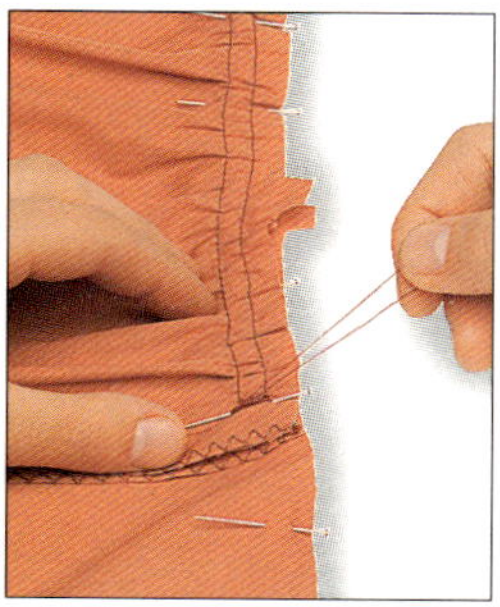

4 △ With the gathered edge fitting the piece to which it is pinned, wind the ends of the threads around a pin.

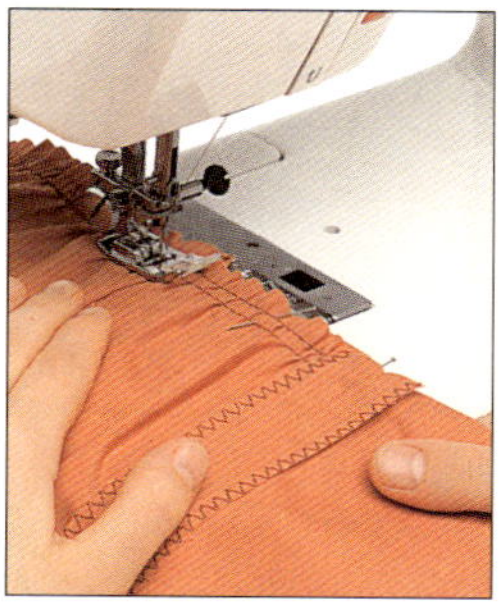

5 △ Arrange gathers evenly and pin. Reset machine stitch length to normal. Stitch on seamline over gathers.

6 △ Remove each pin as you stitch. Trim and zigzag stitch to finish. Press gathered seam to lie away from the gathers.

USE STEAM IRON TIP

51 PRESSING GATHERS

To press gathers, open out the two sections and press the seam flat as it should lie in the finished garment. Work the tip of the iron into the opened-out gathers rather than over the folds. Iron on the wrong side of the fabric.

52 TYPES OF PLEAT

Pleats are commonly used on dresses or skirts to take in fullness at the waist. You can edgestitch to hold the creases in position, or topstitch from waist to hip. The pleats can be pressed crisply or left to hang as soft folds.

◁ ***Plain knife pleats** are the most common pleat. Each pleat is formed with a single foldline and placement line. When folded, each pleat faces in the same direction.*

◁ ***Box pleats** are an attractive decorative feature in which each pleat has two folds facing away from each other on the right side. The back folds may meet on the wrong side.*

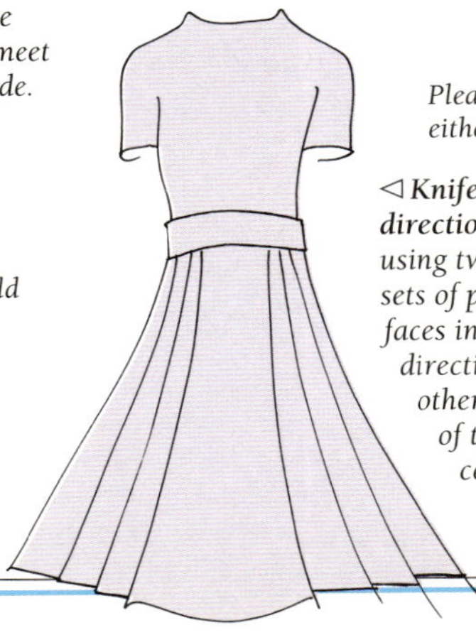

◁ ***Knife pleats in two directions** are formed using two different sets of pleats. Each set faces in the opposite direction to the other, on either side of the garment center front and center back.*

53 FORMING PLEATS: RIGHT SIDE

Use the right side of the fabric to form plain knife pleats, especially if using a patterned or plaid piece of fabric that needs careful pleating to position motifs. Secure the basted pleats at the top with a seam or waistband. You can partially stitch them down flat with a topstitch from waist to hip, or give them an edgestitched finish.

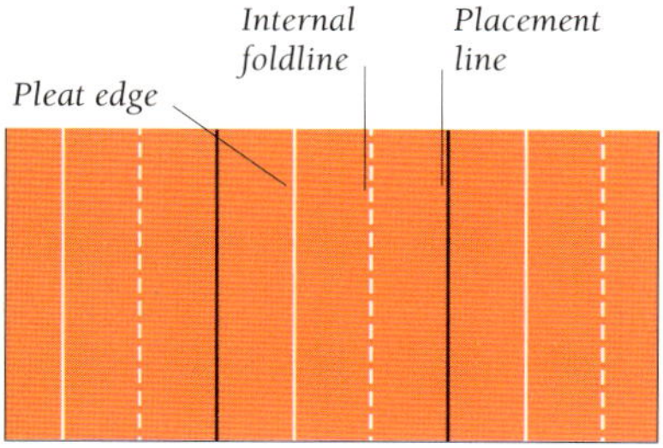

1 △ Pin the paper pattern on the right side of the fabric. Use tailor's tacks (*Tip 33*) and two colors of thread, marking front foldlines with one color and placement lines with another.

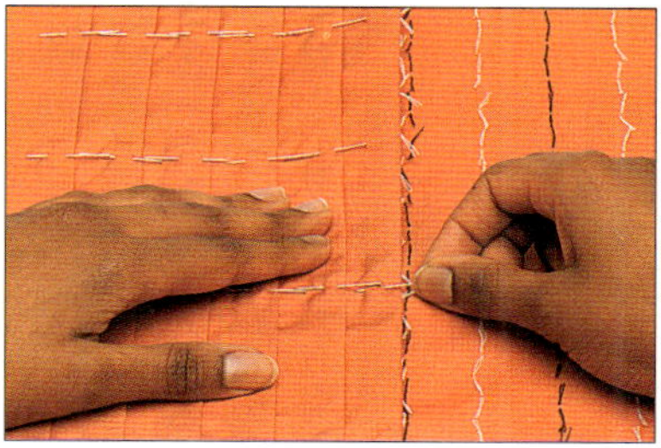

2 △ Cut tailor's tacks and remove pattern. Fold fabric along foldline (with right side facing). Place folded edge on the placement line. Pin through all thicknesses at regular intervals.

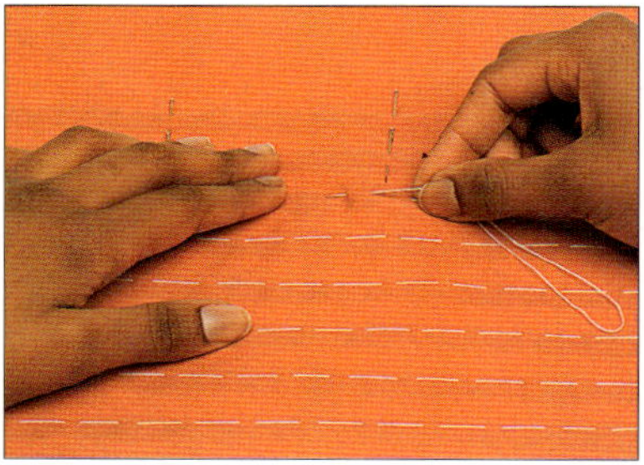

3 △ Check the garment for fit, and remove the tailor's tacks. Now baste each pleat through all thicknesses close to the foldline, removing the pins after basting. Leave the basting in place until you have finished the garment to make sure you achieve sharp pleats.

4 △ Press pleats with right sides facing. Use a damp pressing cloth for sharp pleats, and leave to dry on the ironing board. Turn the fabric over and press with pressing cloth from the wrong side. Use thin cardboard to prevent ridges from forming on the right side.

54 FORMING PLEATS: WRONG SIDE

Certain pleats need to be formed on the wrong side of the fabric. These include inverted pleats, which have two foldlines and a single placement line, pleats that need stitching on the wrong side, and pleats that need matching with other pattern pieces. Start by getting the paper pattern on the right side of the fabric.

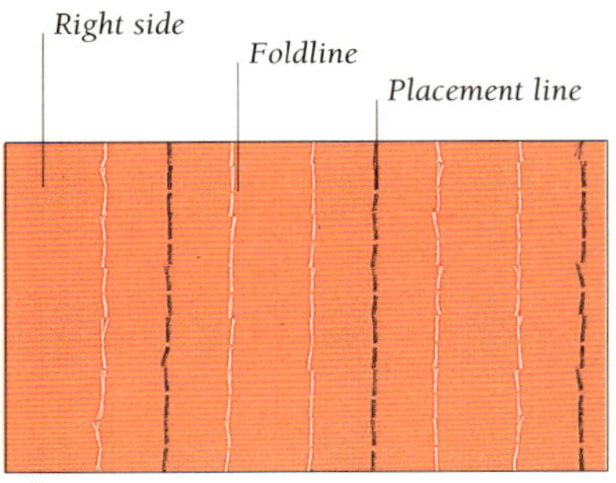

1 △ Using tailor's tacks (*Tip 33*), mark all the placement lines and foldlines for the pleats. Have a different color for each line. Then cut the tailor's tacks and remove the pattern.

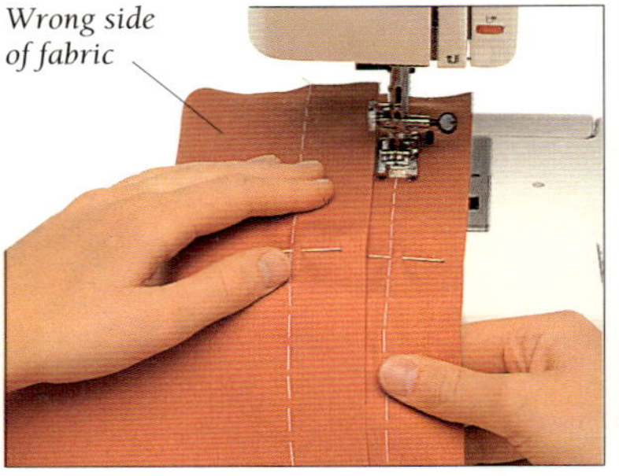

2 △ Fold along each placement line and match each set of foldlines. Pin and baste every pleat. If necessary, machine stitch between hip and waist. Unfold the pleats.

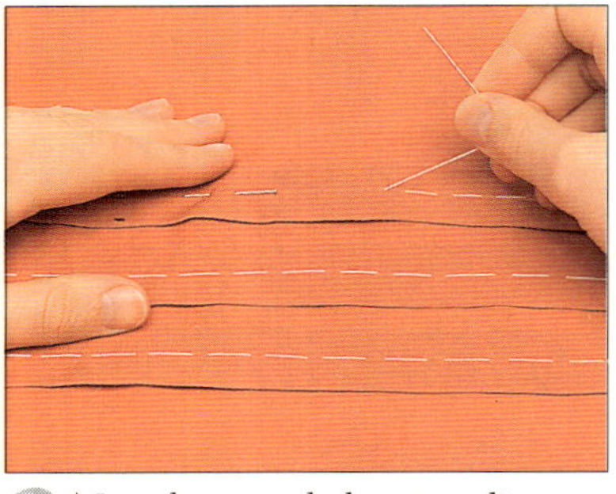

3 △ Lay the central placement line over the joined foldlines. Pin and baste along the center of each pleat. Check the position of the pleats on the right side of the garment.

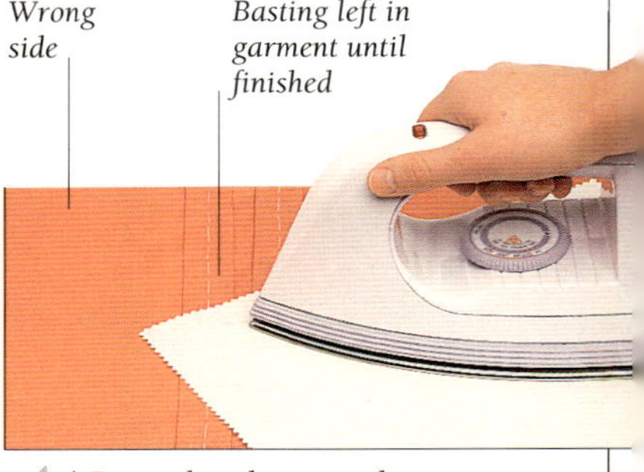

4 △ Press the pleats on the wrong side. Use a damp cloth for crisp pleats and allow to dry. Iron lightly over a dry cloth for soft pleats. Turn to the right side, press and check positions.

WAISTBANDS

55 CHOOSING A WAISTBAND

Straight waistbands provide a stable and neat finish for skirts and pants. They must fit snugly and be firm enough to allow the garment to hang well from it.

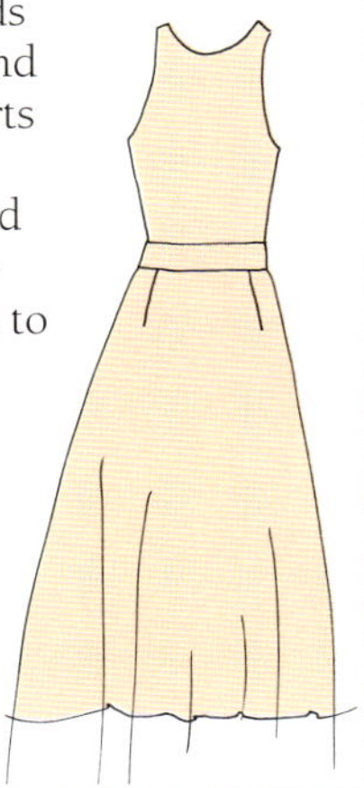

BASIC WAISTBAND
This popular style suits many types of dress and skirt. It is usually 1–1½in (2.5–4cm) wide and fine for most fabrics.

56 REINFORCING

To stiffen a waistband to prevent stretching or buckling, use an interfacing (*Tip 69*), or you can try a special fusible stiffening with set widths and slots marking the stitching lines and foldlines.

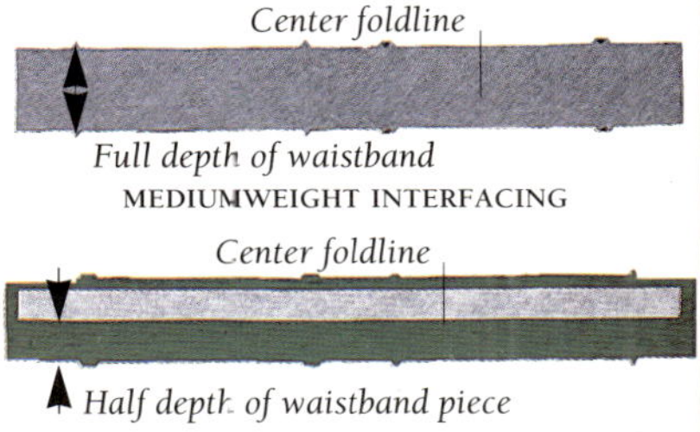

57 PINNING IN PLACE

Waistbands are attached after a garment is finished. Cut out the waistband piece to the length and width of your paper pattern. Apply the stiffening, or interfacing, to the wrong side of the waistband piece. With right sides together and raw edges of a pattern (if being used) even, place the waistband piece on the waist edge. Match the waistband notches to the garment waist edge, and pin notches on the waistband piece to the waist edge.

WAISTBAND LENGTH
Both ends of a waistband extend past the zipper edges to allow for seam allowances at each end and for underlap or overlap.

58 MAKING A BASIC WAISTBAND

It is common to combine hand- with machine stitching to make a waistband. Machine stitch one long edge of the waistband to the garment's right side. Press the other long edge under, then fold the waistband in half. Handstitch this edge to the garment's wrong side.

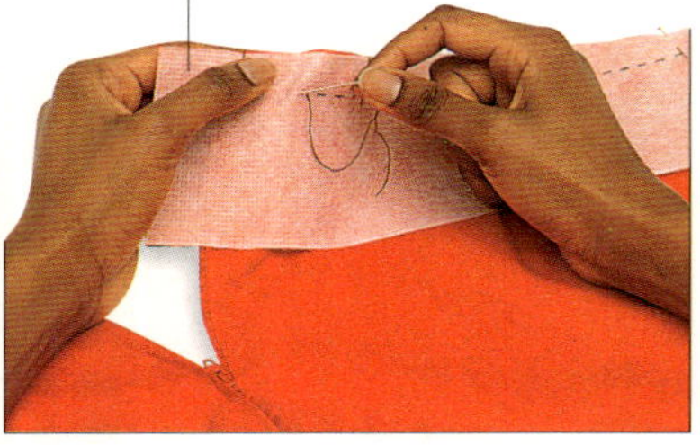

1 △ Fuse or tack the interfacing on the wrong side of the waistband. Pin the waistband to the waist edge with the right sides together and the pattern markings matching. Baste in place, and remove the pins. Stitch together.

2 △ Remove basting and trim seam allowances, layering them (*Tip 38*) if necessary. Press waistband and seam allowances away from garment. Press the allowance to the wrong side on the other long edge of the waistband.

3 △ Trim. Then fold the waistband ends in half with right sides together. Pin across the waistband ends and machine stitch. Trim seam allowances and the top corners diagonally.

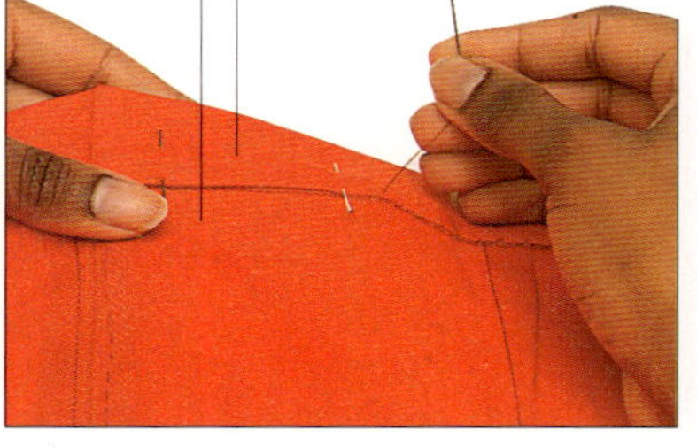

4 △ Turn the waistband right side out. Align, pin, and press the pressed edge with the inner stitching. Slipstitch underlap/overlap lower edges together. Handstitch pressed edge to stitching.

59 MACHINE-FINISHED WAISTBAND

Stitch the outer edge of the waistband to the right side of the garment, as for Tip 58. After finishing the waistband ends, and turning the waistband right side out, press the inner long edge flat over the seam on the inside. Then stitch from the right side along the waistband seam to make a stitch-in-the-ditch seam.

Right side of waistband

Zigzag stitch along edge

1 ▷ Apply interfacing to the wrong side of the waistband. With the right sides together, pin and stitch waistband to waist edge. Press the waistband away from the garment. Trim ¼in (6mm) from the other long edge, and zigzag stitch along the trimmed edge.

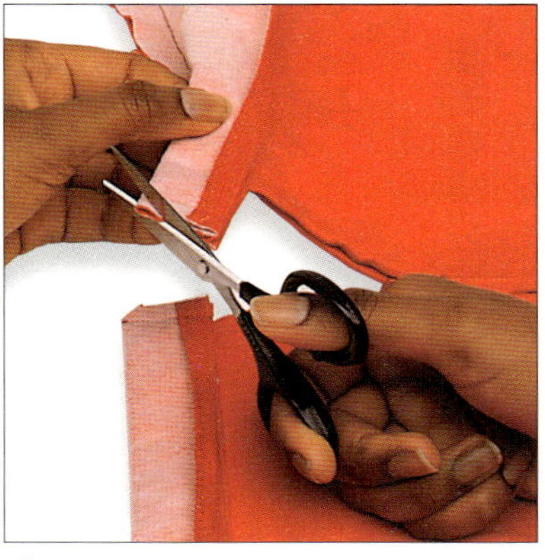

2 △ Press ⅜in (1cm) to the wrong side of the waistband at each end of the zigzag stitched edge. Fold both ends in half, with right sides together. Machine stitch (*Tip 58*). Trim the ends and top corners. Turn waistband right side out.

3 △ Press the band so the zigzag-stitched edge overlaps the seamline inside. On the right side, pin lower edges of underlap and around waistband seam-line. Stitch across underlap edges and stitch-in-the-ditch around waistband.

60 ADDING ELASTIC TO A WAISTBAND

This method is suitable for knit fabrics and for garments with or without waist darts. The pants or skirt should be sewn but not hemmed before you attach the elastic waistband. Use corded elastic, which is hardwearing and braided and has a strong grip.

1 △ Cut the waistband piece on the straight grain of the fabric. Join the waistband ends with the right sides together. Press the seam open. Cut elastic to fit the waist, adding 1in (2.5cm). Overlap and stitch elastic ends.

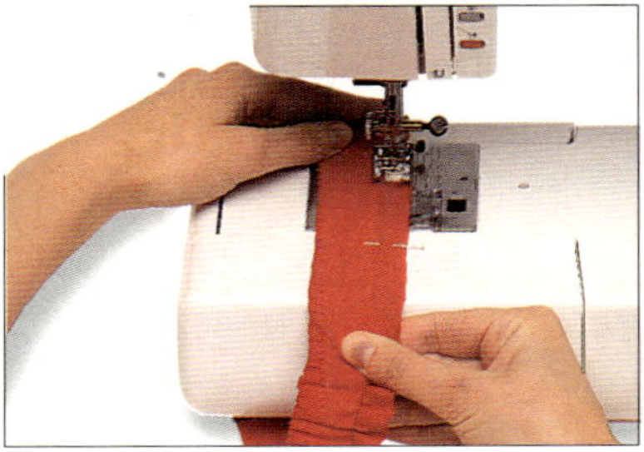

2 △ Divide the garment edges and waistband into quarters, and mark with pins. Fold the waistband lengthwise in two enclosing the elastic loop, wrong sides together. Machine baste just inside the seamline allowance.

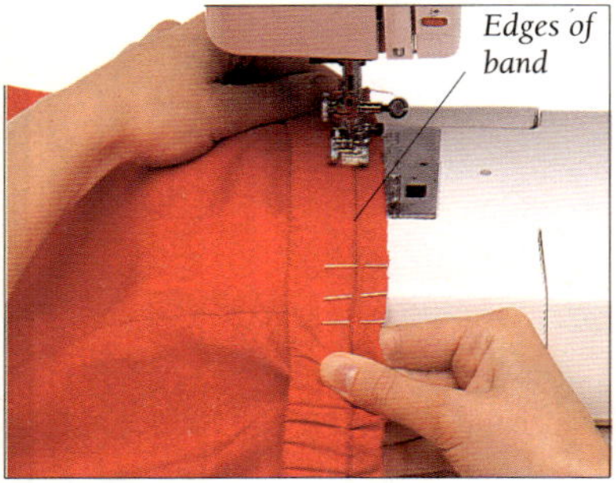

3 △ Pin the waistband to the right side of the garment with the quarters matching. Stitch just inside the machine basting, stretching the waistband between the pins. Trim and neaten the seam allowances.

4 △ Distribute the gathers evenly around the waistband. Stitch-in-the-ditch down the side seams and center back of the garment, to hold the elastic and stop it from rolling. Topstitch if this is required.

MAKING HEMS

61 MARKING A HEMLINE

Hems are usually the last thing you stitch on a garment. Stick to a simple turned-up hem (*Tip 62*), which you clean finish and handstitch in place with catchstitching (*Tip 65*). Mark the hemline accurately. Lay the fabric flat, or hang it by trying it on with the underwear, belt, and shoes you would wear with it. Pin and check hemline before trimming.

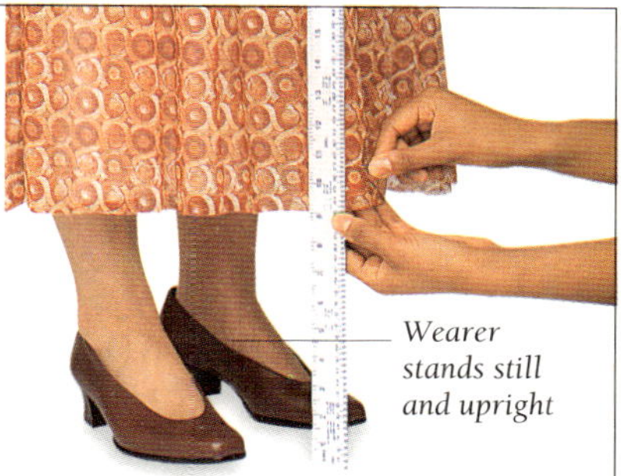

Wearer stands still and upright

WITH A HELPER
Ask a friend to pin-mark along the hemline at 2in (5cm) spaces, from the floor up, with a measuring stick or ruler.

62 TURN UP & TRIM HEM ALLOWANCE

Before you finish and stitch the hemline, you must turn up, pin, and trim the hem allowance. For a smooth, continuous hem, align the grainline at both the center front and center back, and the side seams, with the same grainlines and seams on the hem allowance.

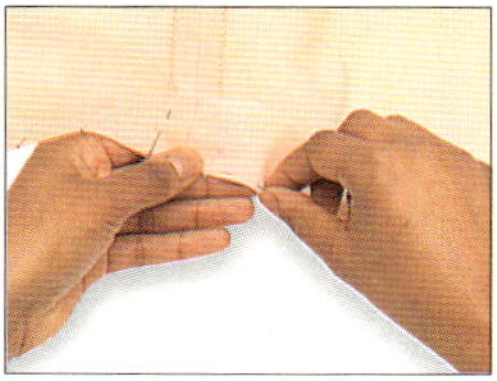

1 Trim vertical seam allowances to half their width. Fold up the hem along the marked hemline. Pin crosswise and baste near the fold.

2 Use chalk pencil or pins to mark an even hem allowance, and trim any excess. If required, easestitch raw edges ¼in (6mm) in from edge.

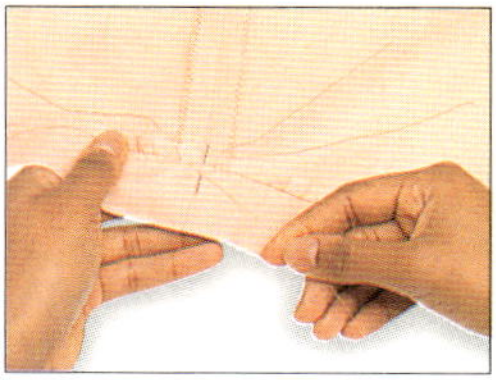

3 Pull the thread ends to gather in the hem until it fits smoothly. Finish the edge, press lightly, and stitch the hem (*Tip 63*).

63 Hemline stitches

Hem stitches are not just for hems.

- Slipstitches and hemstitches can also be used for the inside edges of collars and cuffs.
- Catchstitches (*Tip 64*) are used for joining the edges of facings and interfacings to the inside of a garment.
- Blind stitches or blind catch-stitches can join two fabric layers.

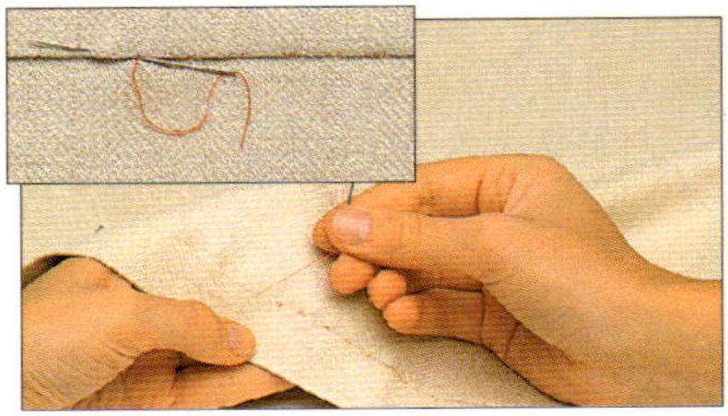

△ Slipstitch
To attach a folded edge to another layer, bring needle out through folded edge. Pick up thread from fabric underneath. Take a ¼in (6mm) stitch left to right through edge.

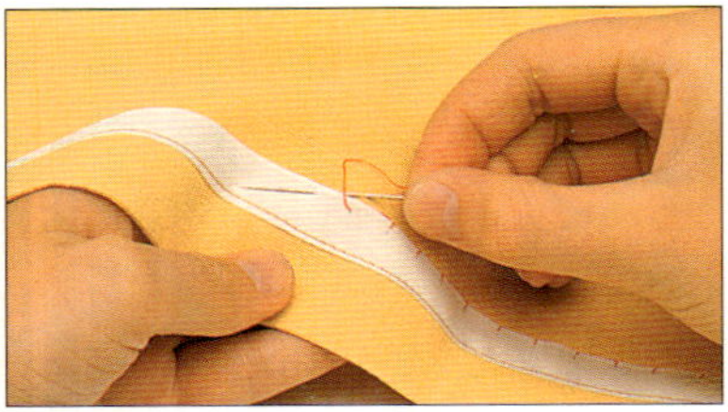

△ Vertical Hemstitch
Bring needle out through hem edge, and pick up thread directly from where it emerged. Bring needle through hem at an angle.

△ Slanting Hemstitch
Quicker than vertical: form the stitches in the same way, but pick up a thread to the left of where the thread emerged from hem.

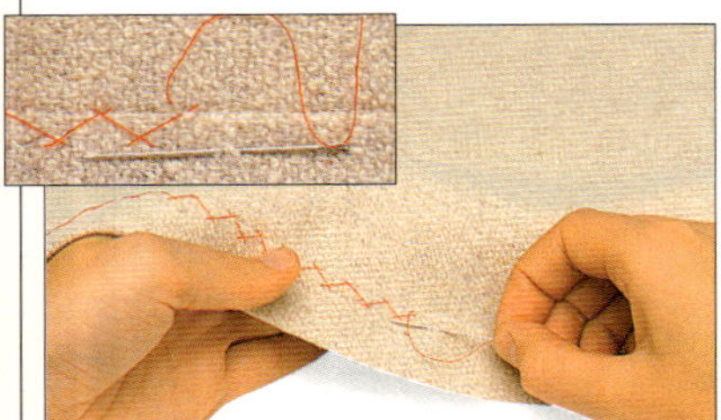

WORK FROM RIGHT TO LEFT

64 Catchstitch

This is ideal for securing hems on heavy fabrics and stretch fabrics. Bring the needle out through the hem. Move to the right, and stitch through the underneath fabric from right to left. Move to the right and stitch in the same way, but this time through the hem allowance. A blind catchstitch is worked on the inside fold from left to right.

65 BLIND HEMSTITCH

Fold the hem edge back about ⅜in (1cm). Working from the right to the left, take a tiny stitch through the hem, then put one through the garment fabric. Space your stitches ⅜in (1cm) apart. Continue in this fashion, leaving the stitches fairly loose.

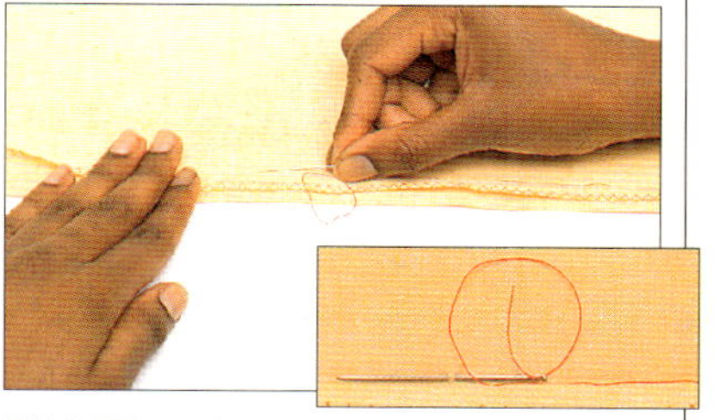

FOLD HEM EDGE BACK UP TO HIDE STITCHES

66 NARROW HEM

Machine-finished hems show on the right side, so a hem stitching line must be neatly parallel to the folded hemline. Mark and trim allowance to ½in (12mm). Iron ¼in (6mm) then another ¼in (6mm) to wrong side. Pin. Stitch on wrong side.

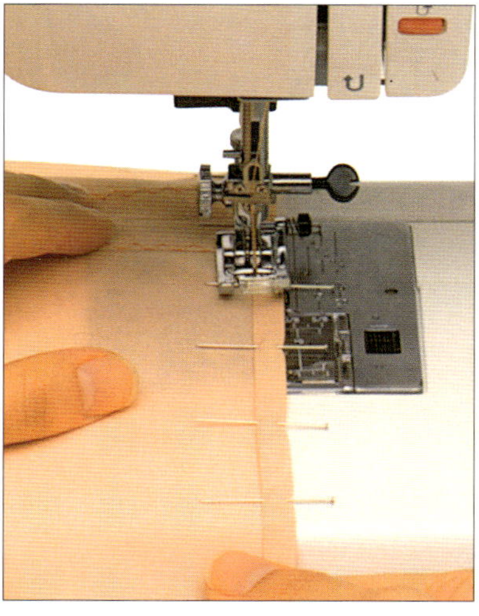

QUICK TO SEW WITH A STRONG FINISH

67 TOPSTITCHED HEM

This hem complements items with other topstitched details. Be careful with all hems not to pull the thread taut, or the fabric will pucker. Mark first and fold up.

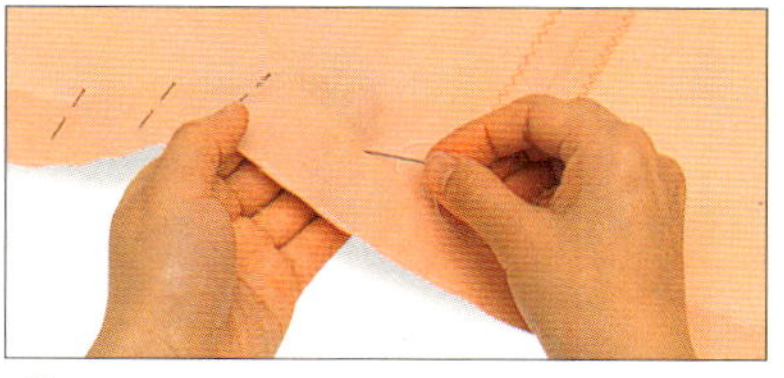

1 △ Pin hem, basting near hemline. Trim hem allowance. Press ⅜in (1cm) under along hem edge. Baste.

2 △ Topstitch on the right side using a straight or a zigzag stitch (*Tip 22*). Use a machine gauge to help guide you in keeping a straight line.

NECKLINES & COLLARS

68 SIMPLE NECKLINES

Necklines are so noticeable since they frame the neck and face. Most will require a facing (*Tip 72*) to finish them. These are usually cut from a piece of the fabric to match the exact shape of the neckline.

- A plain faced neckline is plain on the right side and has no visible facing or stitching; ideal for V-shaped or round designs.
- A single-layer bound neckline works well where a facing would otherwise show through a fabric.

PLAIN FACED NECKLINE

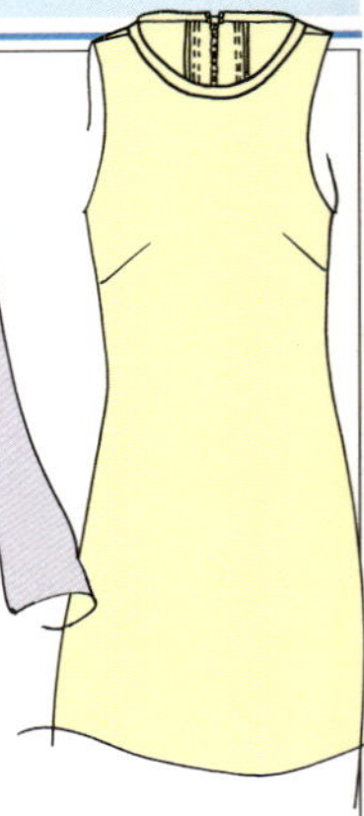

SINGLE-LAYER BOUND NECKLINE

INTERFACING

69 WHAT ARE INTERFACINGS?

Interfacings are a second layer of fabric that you apply to the wrong side to give the neckline edge added stiffening, shape, and support. They can be woven, nonwoven, fusible, or sew-in, and come in neutral colors.

MUSLIN BATISTE FUSIBLE COTTON LIGHT FUSIBLE LIGHT SEW-IN FIRM FUSIBLE

70 APPLYING FUSIBLE INTERFACING

This comes with one side coated with a heat-fusible adhesive, and in woven or non-woven forms. It is ideal for a wide range of superfine to medium fabrics. Test fusible interfacing on a piece of scrap fabric first, following the manufacturer's instructions.

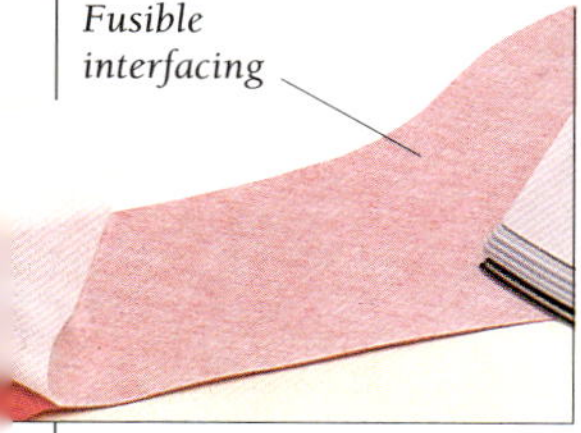

1 Cut the interfacing to match the fabric shape. Lay the adhesive side face down on the wrong side of the fabric. Now begin pressing.

2 Place the iron firmly on interfacing to fix it in position. Do not slide the iron across the fabric. A pressing cloth will help here.

3 Let the interfacing cool. Check it has fused all over. Re-press any loose areas. Stitch interfacing to garment pieces. Trim both as one.

71 APPLYING INTERFACING TO A FACING

A facing is a layer of fabric used to finish raw edges. For a neckline, it is cut to the same shape, stitched on, and folded to the wrong side. You need to apply interfacing to both the front and back neck facings. Stitch both facings at the shoulder seams.

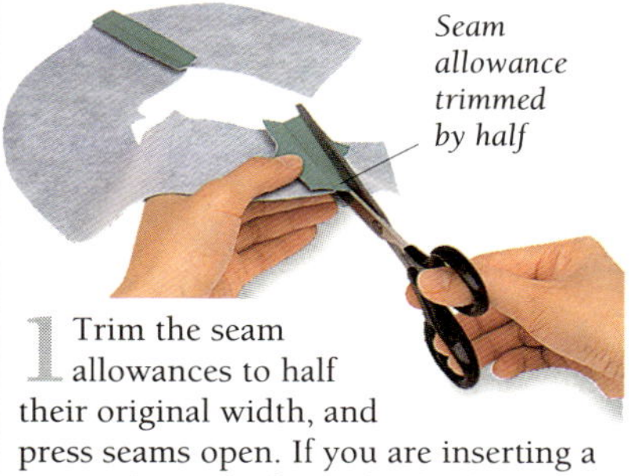

1 Trim the seam allowances to half their original width, and press seams open. If you are inserting a zipper, leave the facing back edges open.

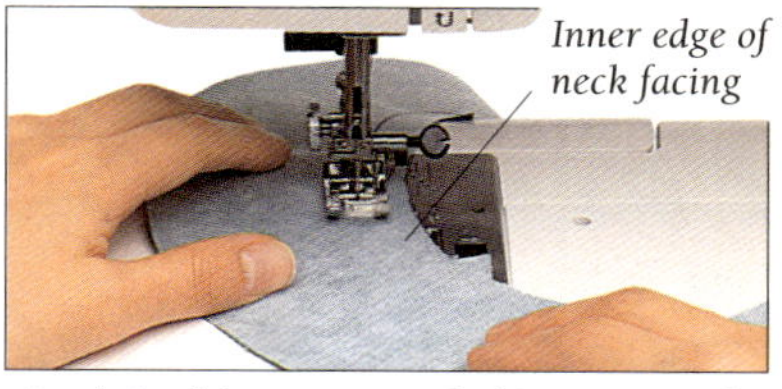

2 If the fabric is stretchable, staystitch around the inner edge of the facing. Use long machine stitches inside the seamline. Replace the pattern. Check the inner edge size, and adjust if needed.

72 Attaching a Shaped Facing

Cut this simple and much-used facing to the same shape as the neckline. The facing is made by applying the interfacing, stitching the shoulder seams, and finishing the outer edge by machine zigzag stitching. Staystitch the facing edge to prevent stretching.

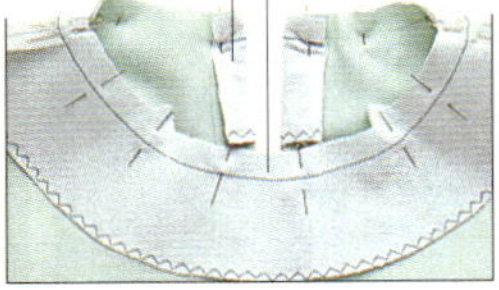

1 △ Attach interfacing to the facing (*Tip 71*). Stitch the shoulder seams. Staystitch the neck edge of the facing. Pin facing to neck edge.

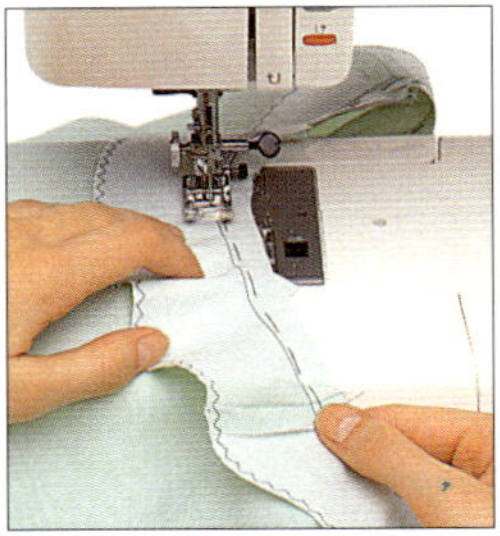

2 △ Baste shaped facing around neck edge. Remove pins. Stitch facing to garment (facing uppermost) along neck seamline. Keep flat.

3 △ Trim and notch seam allowances, then press neckline seam open (wrong side up) with iron tip. Then press seam toward facing.

4 △ Understitch on right side of facing just next to neckline seam through facing and seam allowances. This will hide the facing.

5 △ Turn facing to inside. Allow neckline seam to roll over to inside. Align shoulder seams and press facing around neck edge.

Vertical Hemstitch △
For a shaped facing finish, turn facing to inside, and complete Step 5. Hemstitch facing to garment vertically at the shoulder seams.

73 MAKING A BOUND NECKLINE

When a facing might show through as with fine fabrics, then a bound neckline gives a narrow, neat finish. The binding's finished edge is aligned with the cut edge of the garment. A single-layer neckline has four layers of binding fabric and one layer of garment fabric.

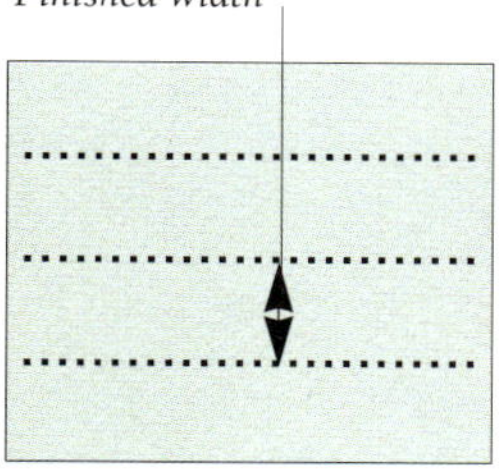

1 △ Cut a strip of bias grain (*Tip 28*) of the fabric binding four times the finished width needed. The length should be equal to the neck seamline length, plus 1¼in (3cm).

2 △ Pin binding around neckline edge. Stretch slightly to fit and stitch binding in place. Work in from the raw edge to the finished binding width.

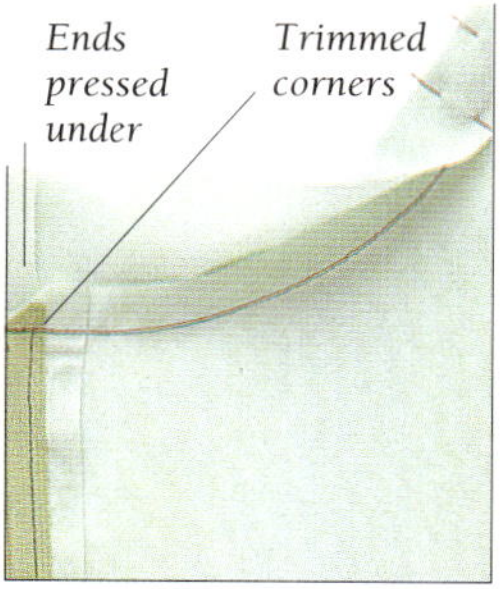

3 △ Trim corners diagonally at each neckline end. Press binding ends to the wrong side, and fold binding over raw edges.

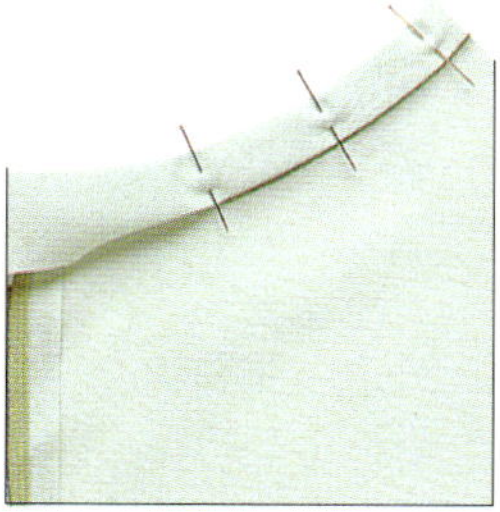

4 △ Tuck and align binding with garment raw edge. Pin binding flat on wrong side of neckline and folded-under edge even with previous line.

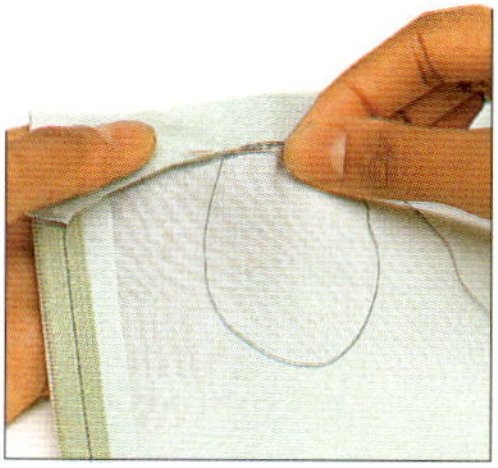

5 △ Slipstitch folded-under binding edge to neckline on wrong side. Follow previous stitching line. Make sure stitches do not show through.

6 △ Press binding so it lies flat. Finish with a hook and eye (*Tip 90*) on the inside above the top of the zipper. Stitch so it is invisible on the inside.

74 Flat collars

Popular for blouses and children's clothes, flat collars sit almost flat on the neckline. Peter Pan and sailor's collars are well-known variations. Flat collars are easy to make and attach.

△ TWO-PART FLAT COLLAR

▷ FLAT COLLAR IN PLACE

75 Making a flat collar

For garments with a center back zipper, a flat collar is made in two parts with the ends meeting at center back and center front. The garment neckline and the neck edge of the collar must fit perfectly.

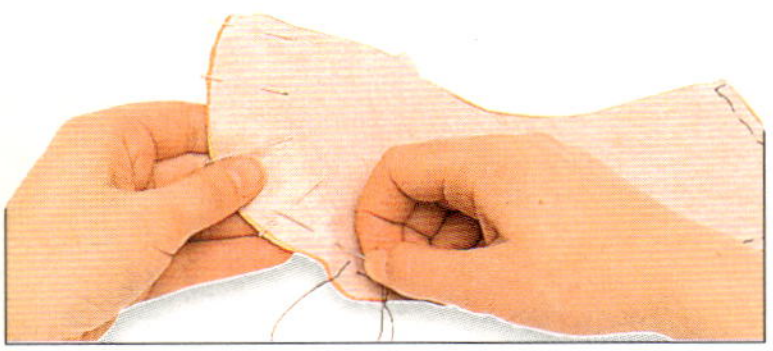

1 △ Apply interfacing to the wrong side of the two top collar pieces. Pin and baste each collar piece to a noninterfaced under collar piece (right sides together).

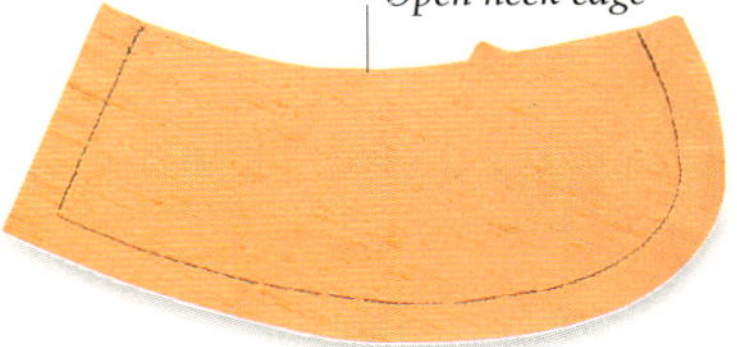

2 △ Leave neck edge open. Remove pins. Stitch around collar pieces' outer edges. Trim seam allowances, and layer if needed. Notch seam allowances at curves and trim corners diagonally.

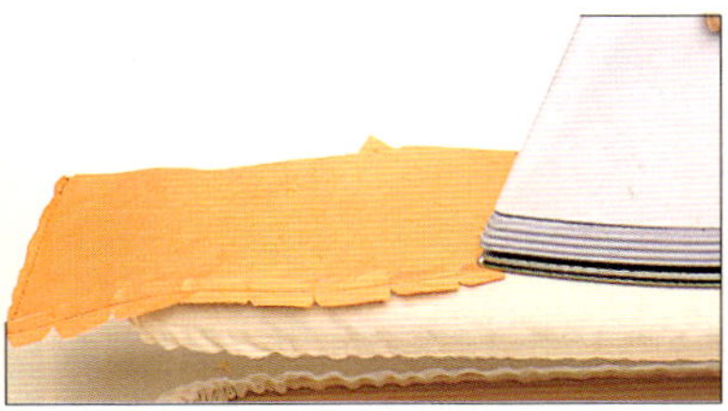

3 △ Work around the seam section, pressing the seam open. Press on the curved part of the board for the curved areas. Press seam allowances toward the under collar, working around the collar.

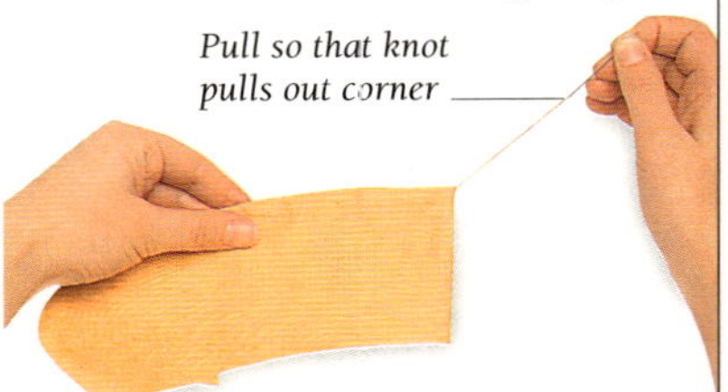

4 △ Understitch the collar seam on the right side. Use the knot of a threaded needle to pull out the corners of the collar pieces. Use fingers to roll over outer collar seam. Iron rolled seam edge.

76 ATTACHING A FLAT COLLAR

Sandwich the collar between the garment and the facing so that the collar will be stitched together with the facing to the garment neck edge. This is the simplest way to attach a flat collar.

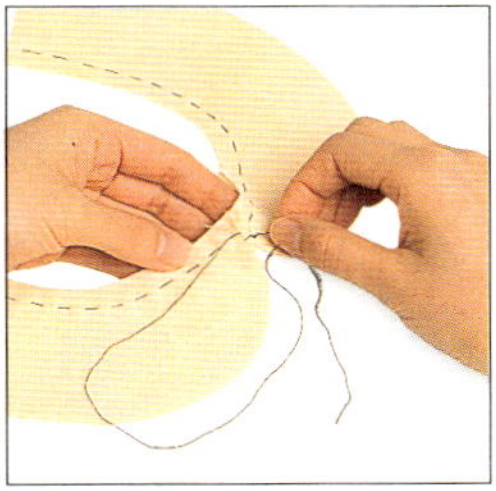

1 △ Baste each collar piece along the neck seamline. Overlap the front corners at the neck edge. Baste together securely so they meet across the neck seamline.

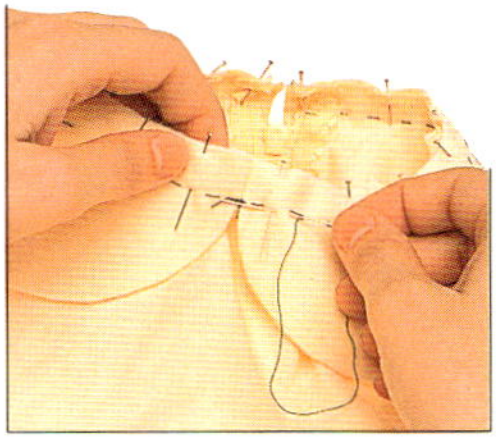

2 △ Pin collar to neck edge (right side) with top collar uppermost. Match where collar pieces intersect with center front pin. Baste collar in place. Remove pins.

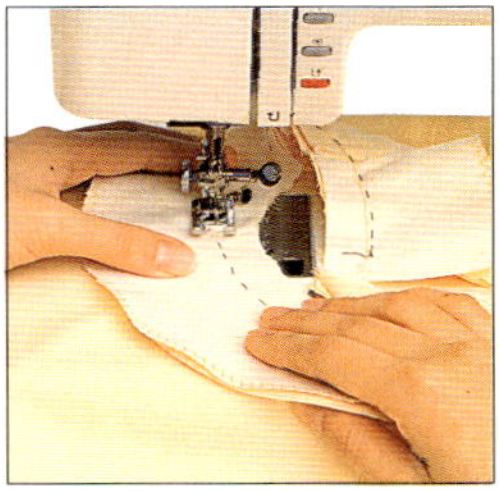

3 △ Sew facing and place along neck edge of top collar, right sides together. Extend the ends of the facing past the zipper, and pin in place. Machine stitch.

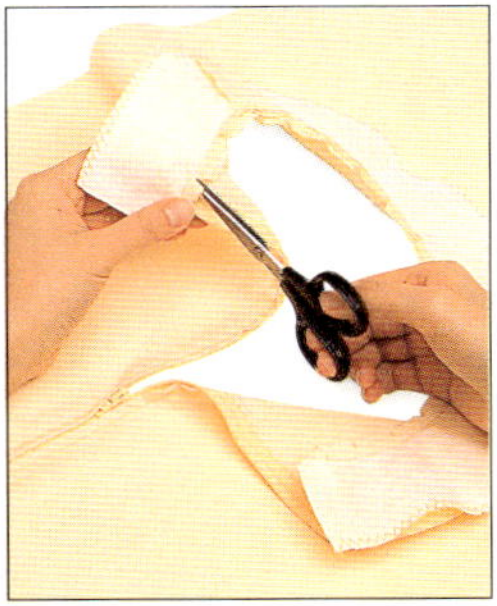

4 △ Remove basting. Trim and grade seam allowances (those of the garment will be the widest). Trim facing corners diagonally. Clip around the curves.

5 △ Press the collar and facing seam allowance open with the tip of an iron. Then press the facing and all seam allowances away from the garment. Understitch close to seam.

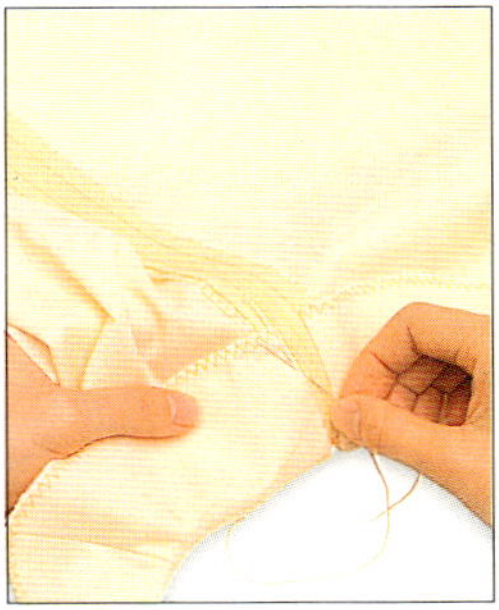

6 △ Press facing to wrong side. Tuck under ends of facing to even them with zipper tape at center back opening. Handstitch facing to zipper tape. Allow room for the zipper to move.

SEWING SLEEVES & CUFFS

77 SELECT A SLEEVE

Set-in sleeves, which are inserted into the armholes, are the most common sleeve. Raglan sleeves are joined to the garment by a seam running from underarm to neckline. The cap is the section at the top that is intersected by the shoulder seam.

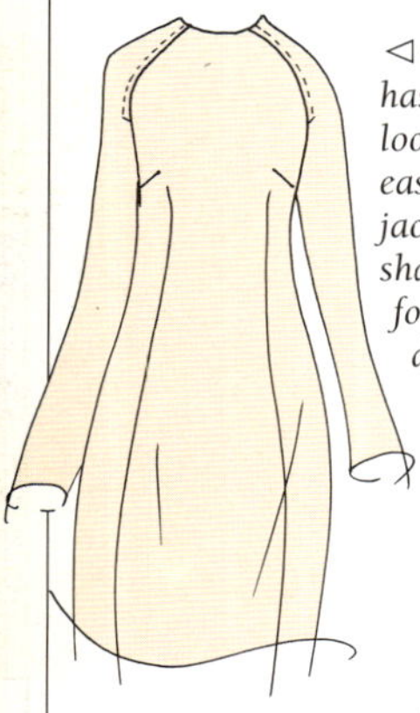

◁ ***One-piece raglan*** *has a familiar deep, loose armhole, ideal for easy-fitting dresses and jackets. The shoulder shaping on the sleeve is formed by an open dart on the shoulder.*

Set-in sleeve ▷ *hangs straight because of its deep sleeve cap. This gives a stylish, tailored look.*

78 ATTACHING A SET-IN SLEEVE

This is cut separately from the garment and inserted into the armhole. You will find the seamline length along the sleeve's top curve is a little longer than the matching armhole seamline. You must ease in the fullness to form a smooth cap.

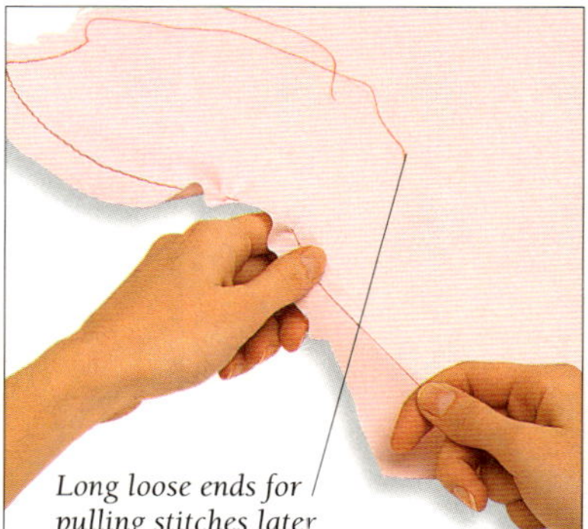

1 △ Adjust the machine stitch to the longest length, and easestitch at the top of the sleeve between notches. Easestitches are long machine stitches, in a single or double row, that ease in fullness where the distance between notches is uneven between seam edges.

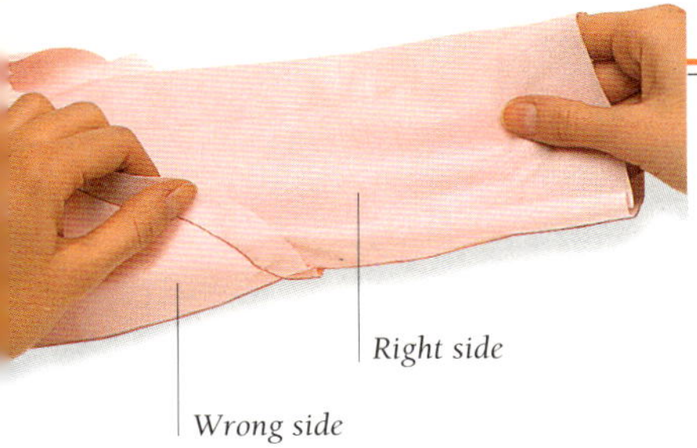

2 △ Leave long threads at both ends. Cut and untangle. With right sides together and raw edges even, pin the underarm sleeve together. Machine stitch the pinned seam, making sure that the ends of the easestitching threads do not get caught in the seam. Press the seam open, and seam finish the raw edges. Carefully turn the seamed sleeve right side out.

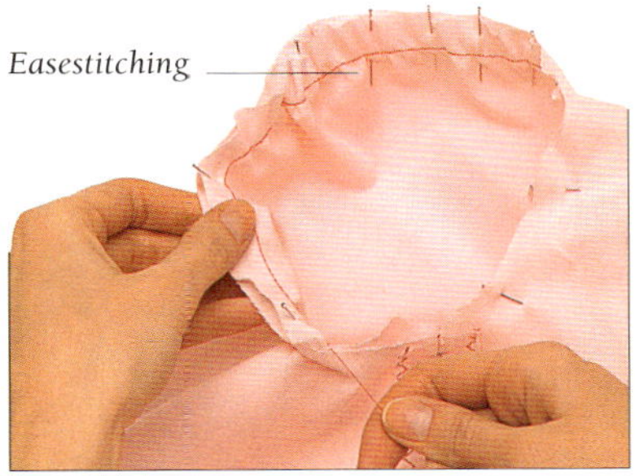

3 △ Put the sleeve in the armhole with the right sides together. Match notches with sleeve seam to underarm seam, and center of the sleeve cap to shoulder seam. Pin these points and in between. Pull loose thread ends and ease fullness without forming tucks or gathers.

4 △ Using small stitches, baste the sleeve in place alongside the easestitching. Stitch sleeve to garment armhole along the basting on the wrong side of the sleeve. Begin and end at the underarm seam, and overlap the ends of the stitching. Remove the basting.

5 △ Zigzag stitch the raw edges together, leaving the seam allowances untrimmed to support the top of the sleeve. Press the seam allowances up to the stitching line. Trim corners diagonally on thick fabrics. Trim just outside easestitching on fine fabrics.

79 MAKING A RAGLAN SLEEVE

A raglan sleeve is attached to the garment by armhole seams that run from the underarm up to the neckline at both the front and back. An open dart shapes the shoulder on a one-piece sleeve.

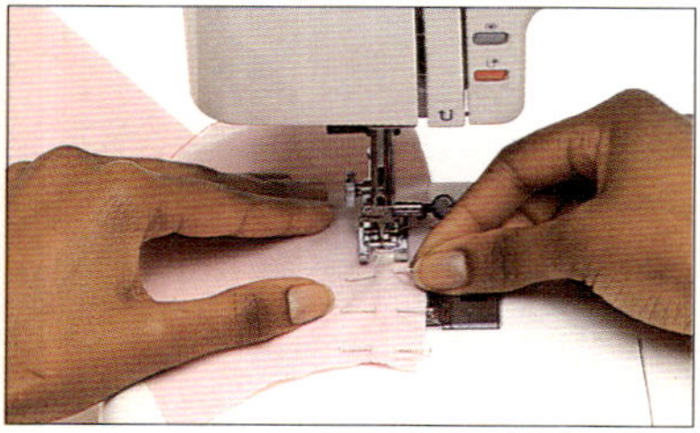

1 △ Pin, then stitch open shoulder dart together with right sides facing and dart edges aligned. Pin, then stitch under-arm seam. Press dart and seam open.

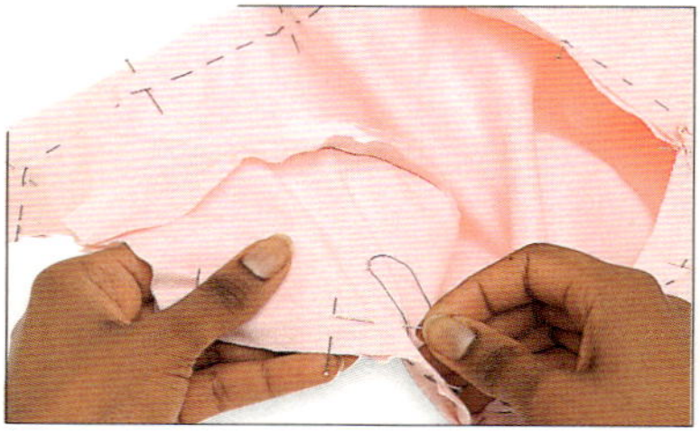

2 △ Stitch garment side seams. Turn sleeve right side out. Pin to armhole with right sides facing, and with edges, seams, and pattern markings matching.

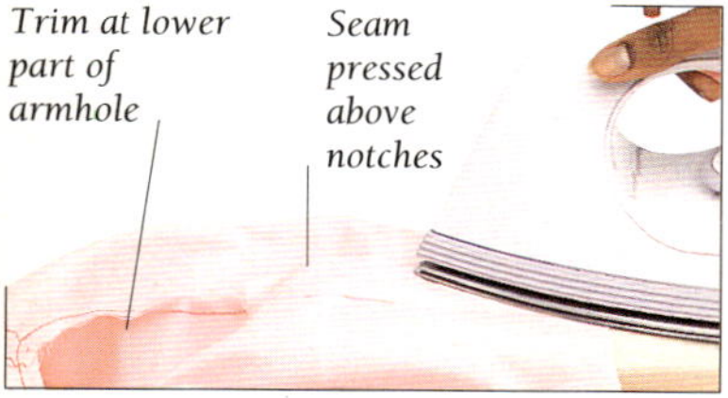

3 △ Baste, then stitch with the wrong sleeve side uppermost. Clip the seam allowance at the notches. Trim between clips. Press the seam open above notches.

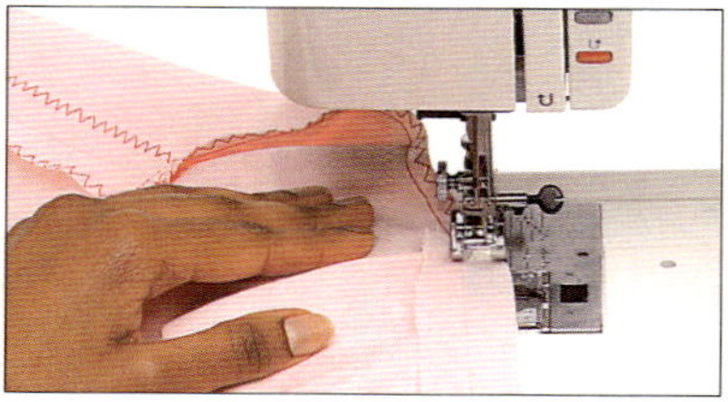

4 △ Zigzag stitch the trimmed seam allowances between the clips. Above these, zigzag stitch each seam allowance separately. Press top parts of seam open.

80 SLEEVE FINISHES

A plain self-hem is the easiest of straight sleeve finishes (*Tip 81*) – and also the most often used method. It can be used with either a raglan sleeve (*Tip 79*) or a set-in sleeve (*Tip 78*).

SLEEVE SELF-HEM
Frequently used on jackets, coats, and dresses, the self-hem sleeve makes a plain, invisible finish.

81 FINISHING WITH A SELF-HEM

Simply fold the sleeve's edge to the fabric's wrong side along the hemline; hand-stitch to the inside of the sleeve. Stitch the hemming down from the clean finished edge for an invisible, flat finish.

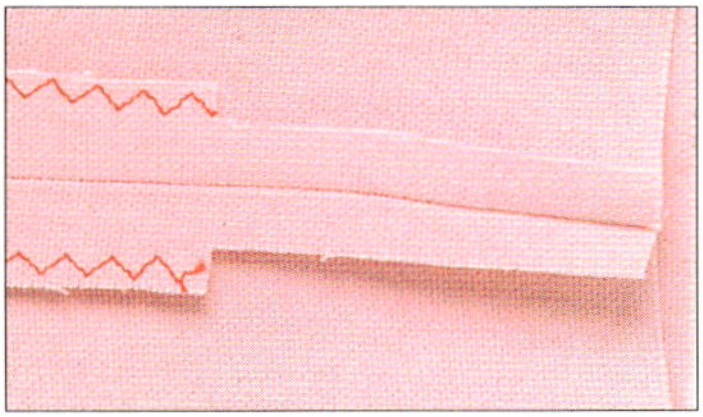

1 △ Mark the sleeve hemline on the right side of the fabric. Remove bulk, if you need to, by trimming the seam allowances by half between the hemline and the raw edge.

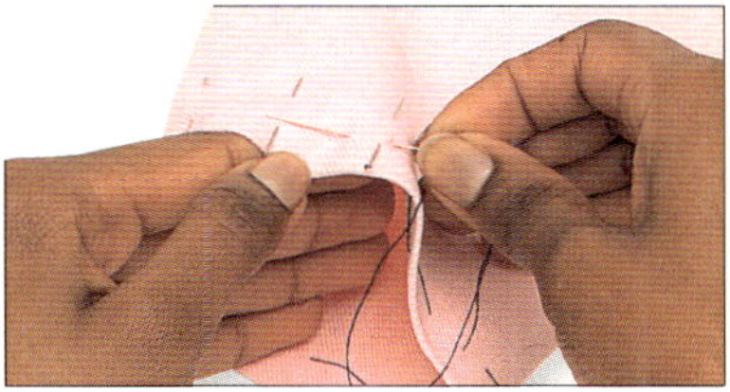

2 △ If an interfacing is needed, apply it to the wrong side of the hem allowance. Turn the hem to the wrong side of the sleeve, and pin near the fold, then baste. Remove all the pins.

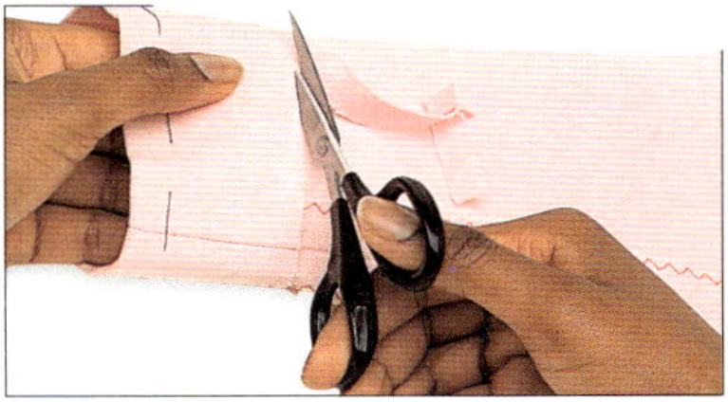

3 △ Measure the required hem depth up from the fold, and mark around the hem. Trim the hem allowance along the marked line.

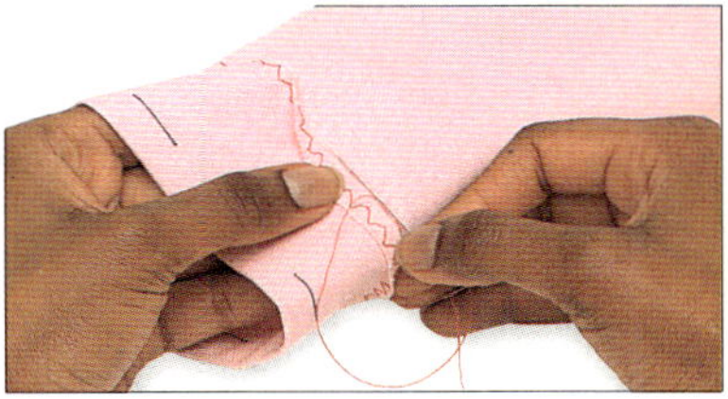

4 △ Zigzag stitch the raw hem edge. Baste hem ⅝in (1.5cm) below the zigzagged edge. Turn back hem edge, and catchstitch hem (*Tip 64*) to sleeve.

TURNBACK CUFF
Cut this straight cuff without an opening as an extension of the sleeve (Tip 83) *or as a separate piece.*

82 AN EASY CUFF

Ideal for coats and jackets, turnback cuffs (*left*) are folded back on the right side of the fabric like cuffs on pants. Cuffs without openings must be large enough for the hand to fit through with ease.

83 MAKING A STRAIGHT TURNBACK CUFF

Use a mediumweight fabric or one with enough body to give you the circular cuff shape. It is simpler to cut this cuff as an extension of the sleeve. Fold it back onto the sleeve's right side, leaving a narrow band to form a shallow hem on the inside of the sleeve.

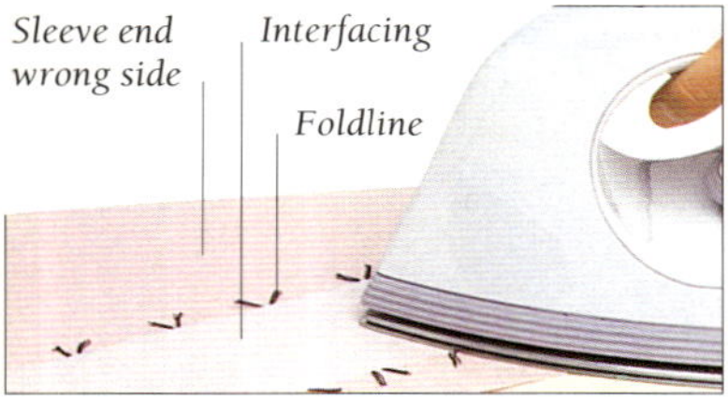

1 △ Using tailor's tacks (*Tip 33*), mark the foldline and the turnback line at the cuff end of the sleeve. Apply fusible interfacing to the wrong side between the foldline and the turnback line. Remove the tailor's tacks.

2 △ Stitch the sleeve seam, including the cuff. Zigzag stitch the raw edges of the seam above the cuff. Press the seam open. Trim the seam allowance between the raw edge and the foldline. Zigzag stitch the raw cuff edge.

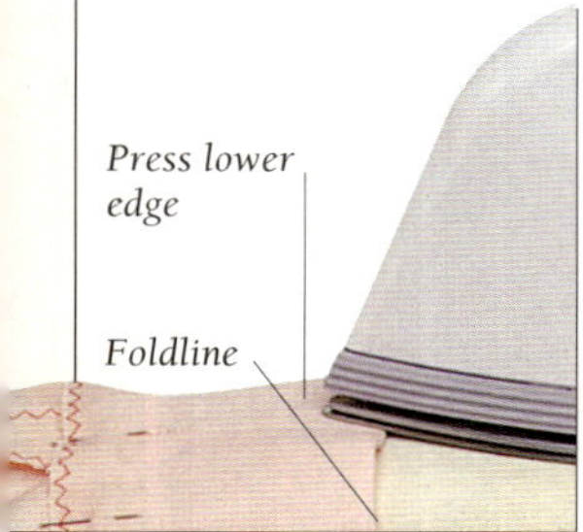

3 △ Fold the cuff to the wrong side of the fabric along the foldline. Pin the zigzag-stitched edge to the sleeve. Press the fold around the lower edge. Baste around the edge and remove the pins.

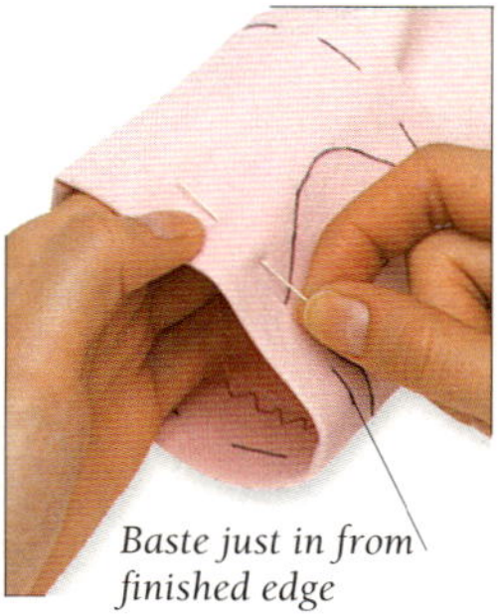

4 △ Turn sleeve right side out. Fold back cuff to right side of sleeve. Press around the fold. Tack through all the thicknesses around the cuff ⅝in (1.5cm) from the zigzagged edge.

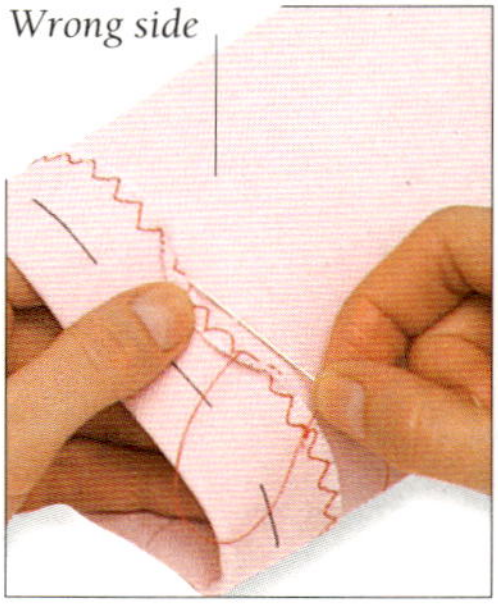

5 △ Turn the sleeve back to the wrong side out. Then blind hemstitch (*Tip 65*) the zigzag-stitched cuff edge to the sleeve. Remove the basting and press the cuff.

FASTENINGS

84 USING BUTTONS

Most buttons are made from plastic, glass, or metal. Flat buttons have two or four stitching holes pierced through from front to back. At the back of a shank button is a protruding stitching hole or metal loop. You need a thread shank (*Tip 87*) for most flat buttons; this allows space for the fabric layers to lie smoothly when the garment is buttoned. You can also thread shanks onto shank buttons for extra movement on bulky fabrics.

A two-hole flat button ▷ *is stitched to a garment with no shank, if just for decorative effect.*

◁ ***A four-hole flat button*** *is usually stitched to a garment using a thread shank.*

A button shank ▷ *is an integral part of the button and lies at the back.*

85 BUTTON & BUTTONHOLE POSITIONS

You can make buttonholes horizontally or vertically, by hand or using a machine attachment. For horizontal buttonholes, the button sits at the end of the hole nearest the garment edge. For vertical buttonholes, stitch the button in the buttonhole center or top.

HORIZONTAL BUTTONHOLE
Overlap edges so center lines match. Pin 1/8in (3mm) in from buttonhole end to allow for a shank. Remove buttonholed edge.

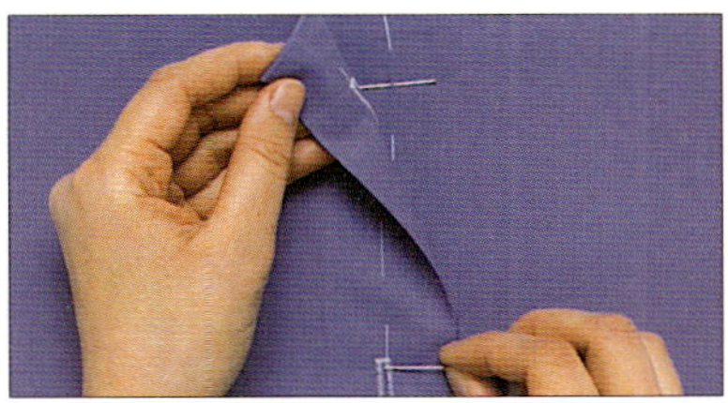

VERTICAL BUTTONHOLE
Match center lines. Pin through buttonhole. Remove buttonholed edge. Lift over pin. Secure pin to mark button position.

86 Attaching Flat Buttons

Stitch flat buttons directly against the fabric if it is lightweight. Use thread shanks for medium- or heavyweight garments to give space for the buttonholed fabric layer to lie flat underneath when buttoned.

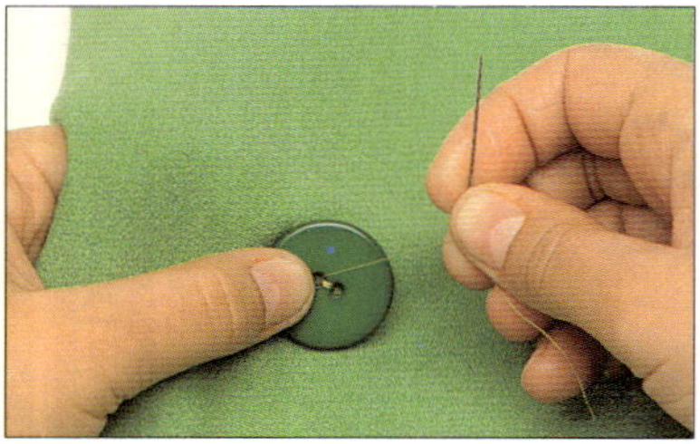

Stitching a Two-hole Flat Button
Stitch from the fabric's wrong side up through one hole in the button, and down through the other hole. Use six stitches.

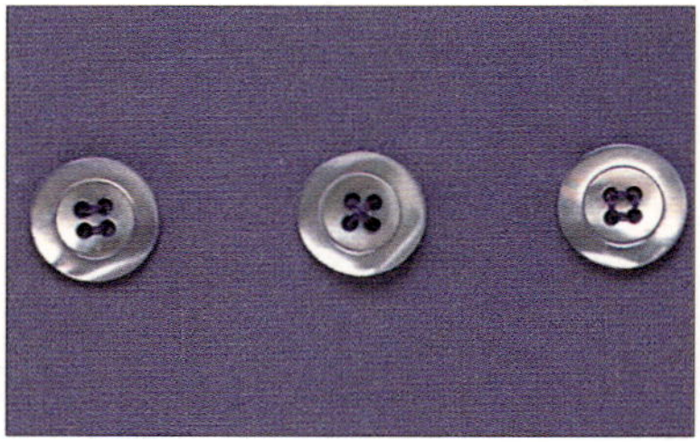

Stitching a Four-hole Flat Button
Secure the thread end at the button on the wrong side. Stitch as for a two-hole using either parallel, cross, or square stitches.

87 Making a Thread Shank

Hold the button tilted slightly against the fabric to make a small gap while stitching on the button. Wind the thread tightly under the button and around the stitches to form a short, firm shank. Fasten the thread to finish.

Thread forms a short shank

88 Attaching a Shank Button

Place the button shank parallel to the buttonhole. Secure the thread using backstitches on the wrong side to stitch through the loop of the shank and the garment several times. Fasten the thread on the wrong side of the garment.

Shank stands away from buttonhole

89 HANDSTITCHED BUTTONHOLE

Always cut the buttonhole before stitching. Choose a single strand of thread for lightweight fabric, and buttonhole twist – which is stronger and thicker – for other weights.

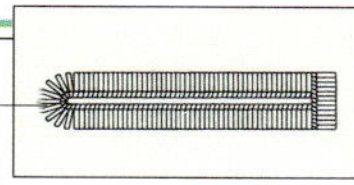

Horizontal buttonhole has one round, one square end

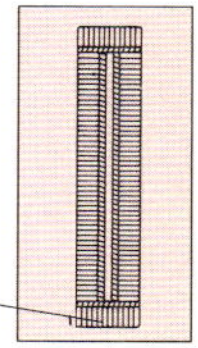

Vertical buttonhole has two square ends

1 Mark the buttonhole line. Stitch a rectangle outside and all around the buttonhole marking. Cut along the center.

2 Overcast the raw edges by inserting the needle into the cut and bringing it out at the line of basting stitches.

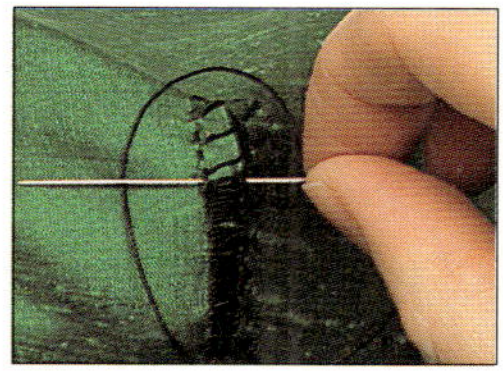

3 Stitch along length of cut with stitches very close. Fan stitches out at corner. Make a bar of stitches at other end.

90 HOOKS & EYES

Often used on waistbands and the tops of zip openings, fastenings such as hooks fit either on looped (or round) eyes to fasten on adjoining fabric edges, or on straight eyes for use with lapped fabric edges.

△ HOOK & LOOPED EYE

△ HOOK & STRAIGHT EYE

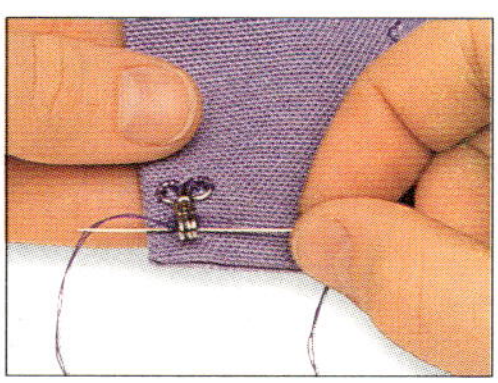

1 Stitch around each hole on the hook, but do not stitch through to right side. Two stitches over the neck will secure it.

2 Have the eye loop ⅛in (3mm) out from the fabric edge. Fasten thread securely. Stitch over each side of the eye.

Adjoining fabric edge

3 Also stitch around each hole to the fabric. Fasten hook to eye. Neither should be visible on the right side.

BALL STUD — SOCKET STUD

91 BALL-&-SOCKET FASTENERS

Snap fasteners (also called press studs) are used on lightweight fastenings. They come in a black or silver metal finish. Small, clear plastic or nylon snaps can be used on fine fabrics. Decorative nonsew snaps are a good alternative to buttonholes, but need a special assembly tool.

SNAP FASTENER
This ball-and-socket fastener simply presses or snaps together, and pulls apart with ease.

1 Fasten the thread firmly to the wrong side of the overlapping edge. Stitch the ball stud to this edge. Do not stitch through the right side.

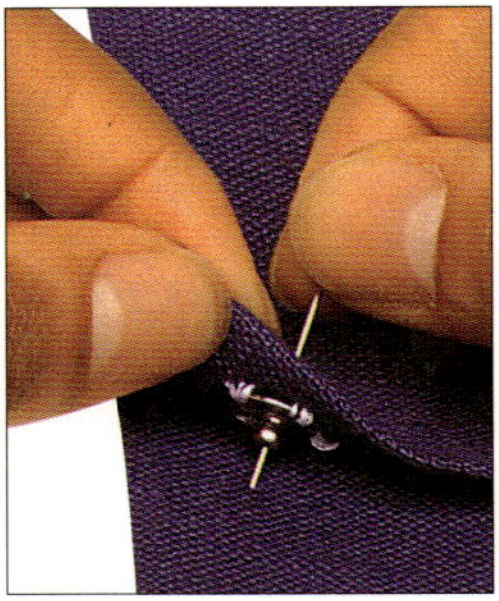

2 Close the opening. Pass a pin through the center of the ball stud to mark the position for the socket stud. Mark this with another pin.

3 Stitch the socket stud (as you did the ball stud) firmly to the underlapping edge. Use four stitches for each hole and backstitches at base.

92 ZIPPERS

Chain zippers have metal or plastic teeth and are the strongest; they are used on garments with heaviest wear and tear. Coil zippers are lighter and synthetic, therefore ideal for fine fabrics. Invisible zippers have a limited color and size range for the average skirt or dress opening.

CHAIN ZIPPER — COIL ZIPPER — INVISIBLE ZIPPER

93 STITCHING A LAPPED ZIPPER

Zippers for skirts, dresses, or pants can be lapped, centered, or invisible. Lapped zippers are widely used at the top of seams, as in skirt or pants waists. One side is stitched close to the zipper teeth. Stitching and zipper are hidden by the overlapping opposite edge.

1 △ Leave a zipper length's opening in the seam and add ¾in (2cm). Finish raw edges. Press seam open. Press allowances to the wrong side along both edges.

2 △ Refold the right-hand edge, working from the right side, and reduce the allowance by ⅛in (3mm) to form the underlap. Press this flat along the opening.

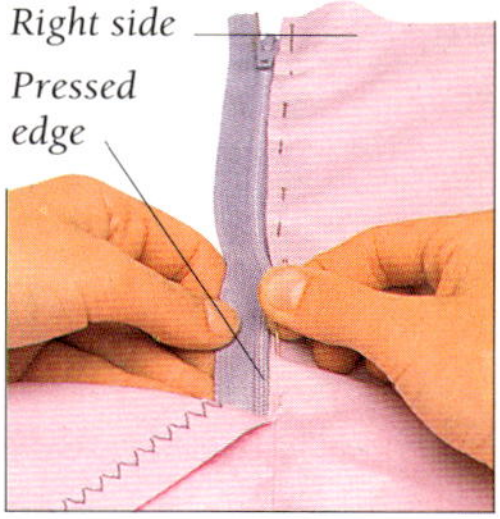

3 △ Pin the zipper tape behind the right-hand edge of the opening so the zipper teeth lie next to the pressed edge. Place the top of the teeth ¾in (2cm) down from the top edge.

4 △ Baste zipper tape in place. Remove pins. Topstitch down zipper between basting and pressed edge with a zipper foot. Stop; slide puller past needle. Finish stitching.

5 △ Remove basting. Put left opening edge over zipper, so zipper is hidden and stitching just covered. Pin zipper tape ⅜in (1cm) in from pressed edge. Pin below zipper base.

6 △ Baste zipper in place. Remove pins. Stitch zipper from top edge, sliding pull tab past needle. Pivot the fabric at the zipper's base and stitch across to the seam.

94 CENTERD ZIPPER

Often used at the center back of dresses, this zipper is put behind the opening's two edges, with the stitching spaced evenly down both sides. Stitch the seam, leaving an opening the length of the zipper teeth plus ¾in (2cm).

USING A ZIPPER FOOT
With needle down, raise the zipper foot. Slide the pull tab gently past the needle to behind the raised zipper foot.

1 △ Baste the edges of the zipper opening together along the seamline. Press the seam allowance open and turn the garment to the right side. Place zipper centrally behind basted opening.

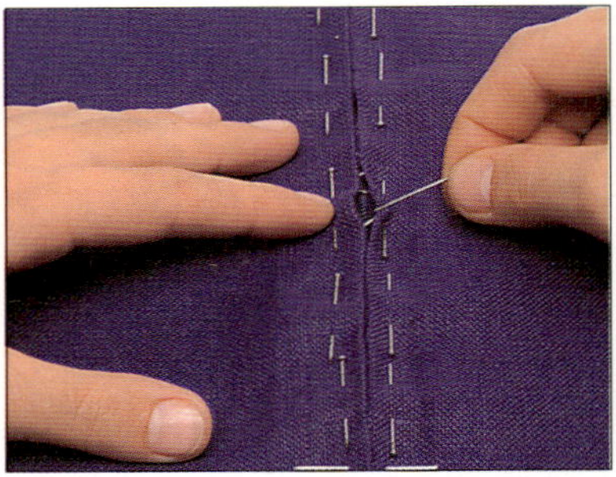

2 △ Put the top of the zipper teeth behind the opening ¾in (2cm) down from the fabric's top edge. Pin the zipper ¼in (5mm) in from the basting. Separate a section with a pin to check.

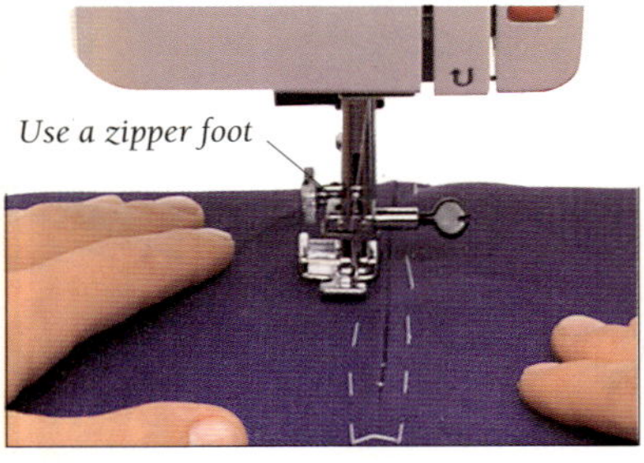

3 △ With the zipper centered behind the opening, baste it in place. Allow a wider space at top for the pull tab. Remove pins. Stitch in the zipper next to the basting, not over it. Stitch to base of zipper, finishing with the needle down.

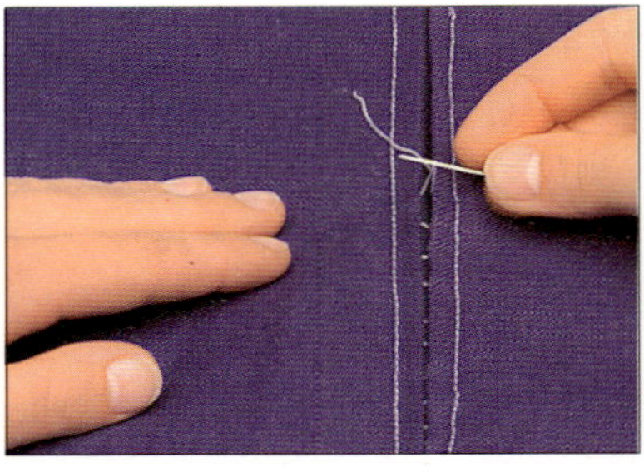

4 △ Pivot fabric, and stitch across the zipper's base, counting the stitches to the seam. Stitch the same number on the other side. Pivot fabric again, and stitch up second side of the zipper. Pull out basting stitches with a pin.

MENDING

95 DARNING A HOLE

Use a long darning needle, a matching thread for the fabric, and a darning mushroom to slightly stretch and support the fabric.

◁ DARNING MUSHROOM

▽ LONG DARNING NEEDLE

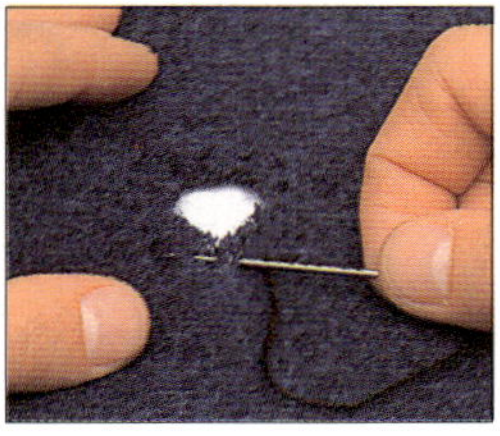

1 Work small running stitches around the hole area to strengthen the raw or frayed edge.

2 Use close, parallel rows of long, flat running stitches over the hole to cover the area.

3 Weave thread in and out at right angles to fill in stitches, catching the garment fabric.

96 REPLACING STITCHING

Trim any loose ends close to seam. Use short, straight machine stitches on the inside of the seam to replace the missing stitches. Overlap old with new stitching at both ends.

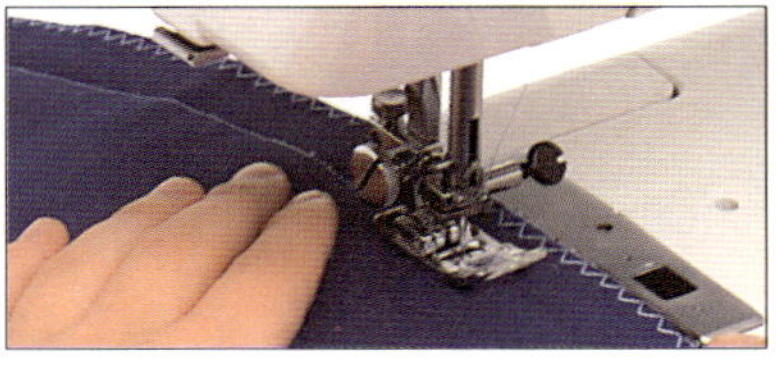

STITCH WITH MATCHING THREAD

97 MENDING A TEAR

The most common method of mending a tear is to use a patch on the wrong side of the tear. Either zigzag stitch across both edges of the tear at once, or stitch over each side separately.

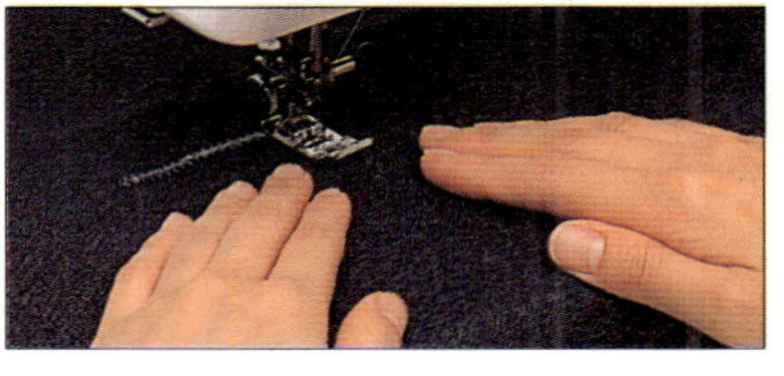

ZIGZAG STITCH ACROSS BOTH EDGES

98 PATCH WITH TURNED-UNDER EDGES

If you can, try to use a fabric patch from the original garment, ideally from a hem or facing. The patch repair shown here is suitable for light- or mediumweight fabrics. When trimming the hole or worn area, be sure that you cut a square or rectangular shape.

1 △ With scissor points, snip a short, diagonal cut at each corner of the trimmed area. Cut out a patch 1in (2.5cm) larger than the hole all around.

2 △ Press the patch edges to the right side. Place the patch right side down over the hole, and work on the wrong side. Baste, and handstitch.

3 △ Turn raw edges of the garment fabric to the inside (work on right side). Slipstitch (*Tip 17*) folded edges to patch. Remove basting.

99 REPAIRING UNDER A BUTTON

Threads holding a button to a fabric can come loose and make a hole. Before restitching, reinforce this hole. For a small hole, use a matching-colored fusible mending tape. Trim to a rounded shape.

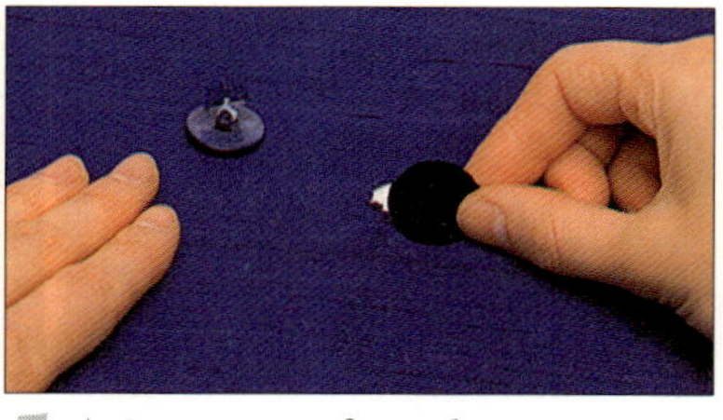

1 △ Cut a piece of mending tape into a circle or oval shape. Using a steam iron, firmly fuse it over the hole on the wrong side of the garment.

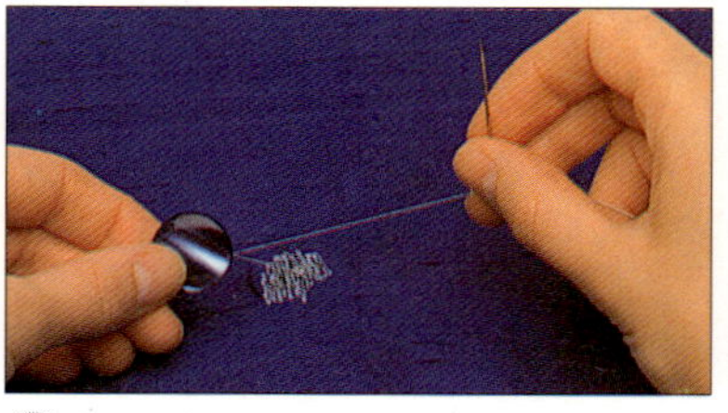

2 △ Work machine or running stitches on the wrong side in rows across, and just beyond, the patch. Stitch through patch and fabric. Replace button.

100 REPAIRING ELASTIC

Try this repair if the elastic lies in a casing and is not held in with the casing by rows of stitches. For a comfortable, snug waist fit, always add an extra 1in (2.5cm) for the seam.

CORDED ELASTIC

FLAT NONROLL ELASTIC

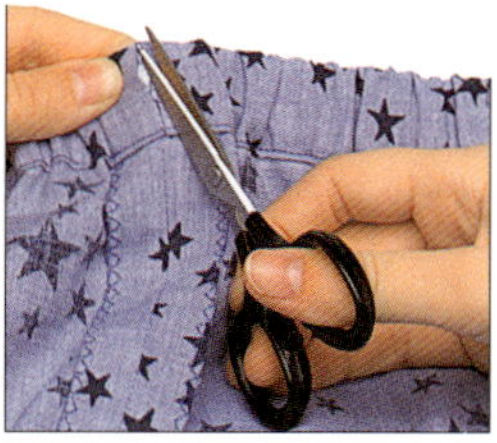
1 △ Use sharp scissors to remove a small opening on wrong side of casing. Cut new elastic piece to fit snugly.

2 △ Cut old elastic and join new piece to one end with a safety pin. Pull old piece so new one is drawn into casing.

3 △ Unpin. Check new elastic is flat in casing. Overlap ends; join with overcast stitch. Slipstitch (*Tip 17*) to close up seam.

101 REPAIRING A BUTTONHOLE

Buttonholes can tear at one end if snagged, or on a tight-fitting garment. Reinforce a worn hole on the wrong side with a small, matching, fusible patch. With care, this repair should be almost invisible. First trim away loose threads or frayed fabric ends.

1 △ To reinforce the area under the end, use a pressing cloth to fuse the patch of mending tape to the wrong side of the fabric.

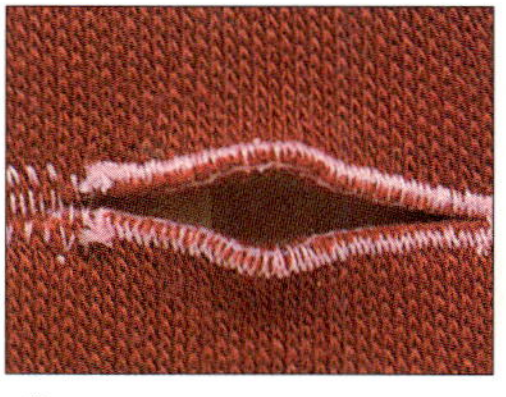
2 △ Work rows of running stitches across the worn area at right angles to the buttonhole. Take care to stitch the fused patch as well.

3 △ Restitch the end of the buttonhole through the patch, lapping the ends of the new stitching over the old. Then recut.

INDEX

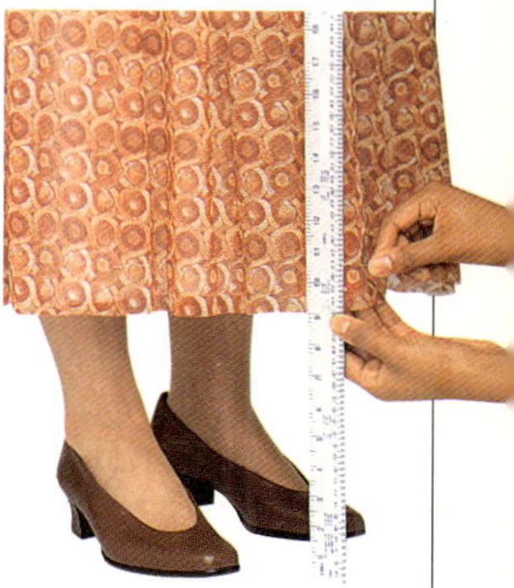

ACKNOWLEDGMENTS

DK would like to thank Hilary Bird for compiling the index, Fiona Wild for proofreading, Richard Hammond for editorial help, Robert Campbell for DTP assistance, Amelia Freeman for design assistance, and Masons of Abingdon for its assistance in selecting basic tools.

Photography

All photographs by Andy Crawford and Steve Gorton except for: Sue Baker 13, 14, 15, 16.

Illustrations

KEY: t *top*; b *bottom*; l *left*; r *right*

Bernhard Gussregen 34, 37tr, 40, 43tl, 50, 54tr, 56l, 58b, 59b; Aziz Khan 21.